# The New Boss

# The New Boss

## Niklas Luhmann

Edited and with an Afterword by Jürgen Kaube
Translated by Peter Gilgen and Michael King

polity

First published in German as *Der neue Chef* © Suhrkamp Verlag, Berlin, 2016

Polity Press
65 Bridge Street
Cambridge CB2 1UR, UK

Polity Press
101 Station Landing
Suite 300
Medford, MA 02155, USA

ISBN-13: 978-1-5095-1787-9
ISBN-13: 978-1-5095-1788-6 (pb)

A catalogue record for this book is available from the British Library.

Library of Congress Cataloging-in-Publication Data

Names: Luhmann, Niklas, 1927–1998, author.
Title: The new boss / Niklas Luhmann.
Other titles: Neue Chef. English
Description: Cambridge, UK ; Medford, MA : Polity Press, [2018] | Includes
    bibliographical references and index.
Identifiers: LCCN 2018006093 (print) | LCCN 2018007714 (ebook) | ISBN
    9781509517916 (Epub) | ISBN 9781509517879 (hardback) | ISBN 9781509517886
    (pbk.)
Subjects: LCSH: Organizational sociology.
Classification: LCC HM711 (ebook) | LCC HM711 .L8413 2018 (print) | DDC
    302.3/5--dc23
LC record available at https://lccn.loc.gov/2018006093

Typeset in 12.5 on 15 pt Adobe Garamond by
Servis Filmsetting Ltd, Stockport, Cheshire
Printed and bound in Great Britain by Clays Ltd, Elcograf S.p.A.

For further information on Polity, visit our website: politybooks.com

# Contents

# Foreword: "Same as the Old Boss?"

## Niklas Luhmann Observes Changes in Management

*Andreas Hess*

Niklas Luhmann was particularly interested in the phenomenon of the new boss and, with his (seldom "her") arrival, the turbulences, tensions, and possible disquietude that result from a change in management. It's an experience that anybody who has ever worked for a larger organization or bureaucratic structure can identify with and will have encountered; and we are not just talking about the very top of a firm's or state's hierarchy, but also further down at the local branch or office. The new arrival potentially threatens the routine and "business as usual," and may have the capacity to destabilize the equilibrium of the organization. In response, management and employees have to rethink their attitudes, assumptions, practices, and work patterns or procedures, and often to adjust their performance and interaction accordingly.

"So what?" one may say: What exactly is so extraordinary about such change? Isn't that just normal procedure? The answer to those questions is that it is exactly the normality in which change occurs that Luhmann's text catches so well. It is the moment of arrival, the first few weeks of doubt, insecurity, and the creeping feeling that change is in the air; sentiments best expressed perhaps in a variation on a line from a classic rock song, but with the famous line no longer a lament or an expression of frustration but rather ending with a question mark that symbolizes doubt over the imminent future: "Will the new boss be the same as the old boss? Or, maybe, will he not?"

What happens next in such a situation? Both hope and doubt seem to be held in suspense for some time and, as the sociological observer tentatively suggests, they are perhaps necessary for any larger institution to motivate people and continue to function. In other words, new energy input is inserted into the system without bringing the system to a halt. In this crucial period, power relations are usually questioned and what is needed is a kind of polite behavior – Luhmann uses the German term *Takt* (tact, or sometimes tactfulness) again and again – to get over this difficult period for all at the office.

At this stage the reader might wonder: First, do Luhmann's observations have any weight in the world, and if so why? Second, why bother particularly with an early text when Luhmann's more comprehensive writings are available?

In the German-speaking world Niklas Luhmann has long assumed the status of a sociological classic. For those readers not familiar with intellectual life in Germany, it is perhaps worthwhile pointing out here that Luhmann and his work have become part and parcel of that peculiar phenomenon called *Suhrkamp Kultur* (named after the famous German publisher), a fact or status which refers to something more than just having a publisher. It means also a good chance of framing public discussion, steering it in a certain direction, or embracing a specialized way of thinking – even though a sociological text might not find as many readers or sell as well as literary bestsellers. It helps perhaps that the German-speaking academic environment still includes an extensive network that has trust in, and pursues the ambitious project of, a comprehensive theory of society. In this context, Luhmann's writings have always attracted attention far beyond sociological circles. Some of this might have to do with the strong phenomenological descriptions he provides, which furnish another view of the world, a view less burdened with normative and/or moral assumptions.

Other countries and audiences, most notably Italy, Spain, and Brazil (and beyond Brazil some other Latin American countries as well), have also been receptive to Luhmann's work, maybe for the very reason that its observational qualities have potentially universal appeal (more about this further down). When looking at Luhmann's reception in the English-speaking world, things get a bit more complicated. The US has been exposed to Talcott Parsons's structural functionalism for a long time, with the result that the contemporary environment hasn't been very conducive to systems theory, whatever its provenance. To many American social scientists such attempts look increasingly like the return of the specter that threatened to haunt their now more empirically oriented sociology departments.

Only since the early 2000s have Luhmann's writings made some headway in the US, and even today such a reception remains a somewhat exotic undertaking. In the UK, the appreciation of Luhmann's work hasn't been straightforward either; after all, this is an academic environment that hasn't exactly been known for its love of grand theory, never mind systems theory. But even here Luhmann's systems theory has made inroads, though to date this has primarily been in the more empirically oriented areas of law, legal matters, state power, legitimacy, and procedures. Again, this success may be due to the sharp and witty distinctions he makes.

Despite such differing degrees of appreciation, it is fair to say that at present Luhmann's work seems to be acknowledged and represented on a truly global scale. His work has been translated into more than twenty languages – with no end in sight: after the publication of his major writings, such as *Social Systems* and the two-volume magnum opus *Theory of Society*, there is still demand for more. Earlier writings in particular seem to be of great interest.

Some of the attraction that these earlier writing, hold for the reader can be explained by the fact that the later Luhmann would sometimes return to previous themes or interests and elaborate on them; the examples of intimacy/love and power immediately come to mind. Additionally, these texts often have their own unique charm, since their distinctions and phenomenological descriptions are richer in detail than many of the sociologist's later writings. Often, such discoveries not only would speak to admirers but could gain traction with other readers simply because the sociologist's distinctive way of observing others' observations (to use a Luhmannian formulation) frequently challenged traditional views and led others to see common or routine actions and experiences in a different, often new light. I suspect that this holds true also for *The New Boss*.

Without reducing theory entirely to individual experience, *The New Boss* is clearly the result of Luhmann's time spent in the environment he describes. He worked as a lawyer in the state apparatus of the German federal system – to be precise, as a civil servant for the *Land* of Lower Saxony, between 1954 and 1962 – an experience that allowed him to gain insight into the functioning of larger institutions and to identify certain patterns and features representative of such administrative offices. The texts collected in this volume stem from the period soon after he left this job, from 1962 and 1965 respectively. The first two texts first appeared in a specialized German journal that discusses developments and trends in administration; the third text was an (undated and unpublished) talk that, given the context, must have been written in the same period.

What makes Luhmann's observations a sociological treat is that they allow us to consider the subtle yet sometimes critical moments of institutional change, particularly as they touch on such decisive issues as power relations, psychological predispositions, and related behavioral patterns. It is mainly through what Luhmann calls tact that major tensions do not get out of hand or can be avoided. As Luhmann further shows, playing on hope, fear, and doubt, adjustment and fine-tuning become crucial to the performance, routine, and functioning of every larger institutional framework; they are vital to both management and employee. In short, they are what gives life to the social organism that is the institution.

Luhmann's early study reveals the secret of

how the organization constantly attempts to re-establish equilibrium while continuing to function – at least for the time being, until a new influx or a new problem demands the next adjustments. It is like rebuilding a ship at sea. The book's great attraction lies in the many fine distinctions made, the wit, and the sense of close observation of such changes. Often Luhmann's dry but on occasion also ironic descriptions match the "empirical" dry reality, including its tragic yet comedic elements that are often suffered in embarrassing silence.

The fact that *The New Boss* is an early work does not diminish the validity of most of its observation. Actually, this potential weakness might turn out to be its real strength, since it avoids the theoretical overdetermination and the tendency "to fill in the boxes" of much of Luhmann's later work. The lack of theoretical finesse is, in a way, compensated by relying on detailed observation that some readers might find more insightful and attractive (and on occasion even entertaining) than theoretical fine-tuning. There are, however, some era-related shortcomings in Luhmann's account, which the modern reader will surely recognize. One relates to sex and gender; the second to what I would call the white and predominantly male "monoculture" of Germany in the 1950s, 1960s, and 1970s; the third to technology and general changes in work patterns.

As pointed out before, Luhmann made his observations in the state apparatus of Germany's federal *Länder* system of the late 1950s and early 1960s before embarking on his second career as a sociologist at the then newly founded University of Bielefeld. This was at a time when women seemed almost barred from top jobs in private and in state or civil service offices. Since then the glass ceiling has moved somewhat to include more women in such jobs, but the situation is still a far cry from fair and equal opportunity, in terms of chances both of occupying the job and of receiving the same payment as men for doing the same job. At present, western capitalist democracies don't feature as badly on the equal-opportunities scale as do some Asian, Arab, and/or Muslim countries (Pakistan, Algeria, Jordan, Bangladesh, Qatar, Saudi Arabia, Lebanon, Oman, Egypt, and the UAE usually scoring the worst), but neither do they rank as highly as some Caribbean and Central or South American countries (Jamaica and Colombia do particularly well, with more than 50 percent female representation in top jobs). Interestingly, neither the US, nor the UK, nor Germany makes it into the top ten countries.

It is self-evident that Luhmann's early text could not have reflected such recent developments. But while the sociologist can hardly be censured retrospectively for the failure to thematize the absence of women in higher positions (or for that matter in other better-paid positions and branches of employment), it seems never to have occurred to him that working in an all-male environment (in terms of top positions) could be an anomaly or, to put it into functionalist language, a sign of anomie in modern democratic capitalist societies. Neither then nor later did Luhmann come back to gender issues or questions of sex discrimination as *theoretically meaningful* distinctions. It remains one of the great enigmas why a sociologist who was so sensitive to making distinctions was seemingly unable to address or discuss gendered forms of differentiation (and discrimination). Even a late work such as *Theory of Society*, which could have addressed the question perhaps under the many sub-chapters that discuss self-descriptions of society, misses out on one of the most important questions and developments of the last and the present centuries.

A similar point can be made about what I would call the monoculture not just of the German civil service but also of larger corporations (and perhaps German society at large) at the time of Luhmann's writing, something which his text simply reproduces or takes for granted. Reaching a top position was then, and remains to this very day, to a large extent a very German, white, and male affair (any look into the recent scandals of Deutsche Bank, companies in the energy sector, Volkswagen, or Porsche will confirm that). Of course, it is impossible to reinject a bit more color and gender into the white whale that so dominated German society and its state and private offices at the time. However, at the least the obvious fact should be pointed out to contemporary readers, who are presumably more likely to work in a more multicultural and less exclusively male environment. Again, for somebody like Luhmann, who made a case for thinking about world society in most of his later work, this early text remains remarkably confined to, and reproduces, the national demographic patterns of the time.

Finally, there is the question of how much technology and modern communication have changed modern labor and management structures, particularly in the service sector, since Luhmann wrote about the interaction and observable changes between employees and management in *The New Boss*. As a recent study reveals, in countries like Denmark, Sweden, and the Netherlands more than 35 percent of all employees now work from home (*Financial Times*, March 11–12, 2017). While this does not necessarily imply a lack of control and supervision, it changes the task of management considerably. Again, it would be a serious case of prolepsis to censure Luhmann for not having anticipated such developments, from regular face-to-face interaction to modern communication presence despite physical and special separation and long distances; nonetheless these transformations qualify the account. What remains, though, and what Luhmann still gives a fantastic account of, is what still worries most employees when the new boss enters through the office door or switches on the computer screen: will the new boss be like the old boss?

# The New Boss

In principle, bureaucratic administration calls for an impersonal style of working. It is able to achieve this by guaranteeing a state of order, characterized by a high degree of predictability. Administrators' daily routines are regulated, and this is the reason that they can keep their feelings to themselves.

There are, however, situations when this does not work. From time to time one of the following situations invariably comes about. Every now and then a government agency, company department, or any given group gets assigned a new boss. This change of manager is among the few exciting events in the routine daily life of administration. You can sense the high level of tension whenever election results are about to be announced and a new regime is getting ready to take over. In such situations, work all but comes to a halt, because no one really knows what to expect, and for a while various rumors provide a kind of surrogate sense of security. When a department head moves away, on the other hand, the broad impact is less noticeable, but this too gives rise to an unusual level of interest in the situation. Problems relating to the issue of who will take over are a popular topic of conversation all the way down to the lowest ranks. Whoever is most in the know is sure to attract general interest and their prestige increases accordingly. The appointment of new bosses by no means resolves all those problems associated with succession. Analyzing their subject and his background keeps those surrounding him busy for a long time. And then there is the problem of the first encounter with the new boss. There is a feeling that first impressions could well be decisive, and social psychology seems to confirm this.[1] It is a matter of finding the right mix of respect and candor, of modesty and confidence based on the repertoire of past experiences, of offering to do things and showing restraint. This is all the more precarious when it is necessary at the same time to engage the new boss in bottom-up instruction and training.

For the new boss similar difficulties arise, the only difference being that his role allows him even less scope for revealing his uncertainty. He is overwhelmed by a mass of new colleagues whose faces he does not yet know. He can only hazard guesses at their underlying motives without being able to decipher these with any accuracy. Added to this is the way that the significance of any initial mistake is prone to intensify, as a result of the concerted attention of those people who surround a new boss and their eagerness to grasp at any possible clues that could lead to their forming consistent views of what to expect in the future.

It is probably unlikely that either the manager or the subordinate will readily think of consulting and enlisting the help of science in this situation. The sciences that they are familiar with hardly encourage this. From the perspectives of legal and organizational science, a change of boss is remarkably free of problems. From a legal standpoint, what is at stake is no more than a decision by a body, with full authority to make that decision, that leads to certain hard-and-fast legal consequences. It is unlikely that defining and expanding on this will take one any further. At the same time, current organizational science understands staff changes, frequent as they may be, mainly in terms of selection problems and training costs. It underestimates emotional problems and repercussions as well as employees' adjustment difficulties. This is because it operates on the assumption that an impersonal, generalized view of someone's role is a sufficient basis to account for their behavior.[2] This is also the reason why Max Weber's model of bureaucracy does not take such problems into account.

We shall have to question, however, whether such a generalized view is viable and, where administrative actions are concerned, whether it is enough just to be aware of the correct ruling for resolving potential legal disputes. A science of administration that wants to stay in touch with concrete behavior in the real world of administration cannot afford to ignore such questions. The issue of a "new boss," which is such a common, recurring, structural event, presents one of the few organizational problems where one can rightly assume the existence of a universal significance.[3] If the conceptual framework of administrative sciences cannot grasp and define such a problem, then this framework must be broadened.

# I

Every social organization can be functionally analyzed, if one regards its stability as problematic and raises questions about the ways that it has succeeded in forming and maintaining itself. In social life, stability is achievable only if the behavior of other people is predictable or, in other words, if each party can rely on their expectations concerning the other's behavior being fulfilled over and over again. This also carries the implication that these expectations are themselves generalized in several different ways. These are: that they are combined into complex types with different options available for actioning them in ways that the situation demands; that they are repeatable; that they are consensual; and, lastly, that they reach the point where they are treated as a norm and so continue to be used, even on occasions when they are factually disappointed. Nowadays, such generalized behavioral expectations are commonly called "roles."

A social organization consists of a multiplicity of roles that mutually assume each other's existence. They complement each other, exclude each other, or are combined together, either easily or with some difficulty. The various forms that role coherence, role separation, and role conflict take are central to any discussion of the way that order is brought to bear on human coexistence. In this context, the different considerations that guide structural decisions both define and identify differences between problems of role-switching that occur in specific social organizations. It is in this sense, then, that the difficulties associated with changing the boss depend on the structure applying in any particular organizational context.

Primitive, relatively unarticulated social organizations rely to a high degree on socially prescribed and lived combinations of roles, assigned to one individual. As a result, the head of the family is at the same time production manager, warlord, leader of the dance, member of the tribal council, and many other things. The successor assumes all of these roles. Social organizations of this kind are therefore able to change people without altering the social role structure.[4] In such cases, the connections between the various roles can be worked out in detail and transmitted without question from generation to generation. The result of attaching a combination of roles to a single individual is the amazing homogeneity and similarity of biographies one finds in these social organizations.

Systems such as these, however, cannot go beyond a rather low level of differentiation. The capacity of one person for different roles is limited. As soon as society develops in the direction of more specific roles and so greater differentiation, role combinations associated with a person have to give way to practical role connections. Consequently, where a number of specific roles become combined in one person, this is increasingly a matter of chance. Practical role combinations are feasible only where the separation between the different roles is well defined, such as that between home and work and politics and relaxation.

This kind of social organization requires social mobility. It provides different careers, with each person acquiring an accumulation of roles more or less by chance. The president of a corporation may be married or unmarried, a dancer or a nondancer, a member of a church, a huntsman, and so on. There are hardly any social rules covering the combination of these roles in one person, and no longer do any general socially acceptable ways of resolving conflicts between roles exist. Every succession to a particular role, therefore, carries with it new ways of combining roles and new problems. So it is that in all differentiated social systems where there is a high level of role separation, changes of role are linked to structural adjustments. It is not just a matter of getting used to new people – every change of this kind also alters social relations mediated by people.

Within formal organizations, there is an additional element that increases the difficulty associated with these adjustments. All organizations, charged with continually achieving certain specific objectives, develop a system of official, formally legitimated expectations. These expectations determine the particular responsibilities of different departments, the channels of communication, and the conditions for successfully obtaining useful decisions. Yet they do not in any way describe the administration's everyday life and business dealings. They only provide a basic reference framework. They are highly explicit. They can be put into appropriate spoken and written forms. They offer a starting point specifically for arguments and justifications. Acceptance of these expectations is a condition for membership of the organization. This makes them prominent and eye-catching. Whenever one interacts with other members of the organization, one can assume that they share these formal expectations. They operate as a kind of "semantic bulwark."[5] Whenever one invokes them, one becomes invulnerable to attack. For this reason, they are especially suitable for dealing with the general public, as well as for written records.

This is precisely why there are specific strategic advantages to be found in the use of a formally regulated language and in attributing certain characteristics to one's conversation partner. The situation becomes public and this partner is treated impersonally as if he could be "anybody" or a possible rival. This excludes any intimacy. One can, therefore, provide oneself with an impenetrable protection with the help of formal arguments that nobody can fail to recognize as such. In this way situations can be cooled down and unwanted confidences discouraged. Furthermore, using these formal arguments allows one to interact smoothly with both adversaries and strangers and express any hostility that one may feel in a way that is not open to challenge. In this way one also avoids being officially in the know about matters that can be communicated only "between friends."

This analysis teaches us two things. In the first place, it shows that formal expectations and role definitions have a specific function in the comprehensive system of an organization and, taken by themselves, do not represent its total reality. An organization cannot live exclusively according to formal expectations. Secondly, formal expectations claim a monopoly of legitimacy for themselves and so obstruct the expression of those expectations that deviate from them. They present a system of consistent, purposive action, free of contradictions. Whatever does not fit in has to retreat into hiding, or at least withdraw into a more limited public sphere that relies on a narrower kind of trust.

In every organization, therefore, an informal order develops below the formal one, with its own roles, with individually shaped, personalized expectations, and with smaller groups and cliques who, within their circles, bring legitimacy to useful deviations from the formal order, form centers of power, and support their members in all sorts of conflicts. Typically, informal modes of organization are not directed toward specific objectives, but are rather oriented around specific people. Their focal points are those needs that the formal order either does not satisfy or constructs through its own one-sidedness.

While as a result their "issues" are to a large degree predetermined by the formal mode of organization, there are self-sustaining norms and institutions in the informal field that do not have any obvious relation to the formal ordering. They can damage it as well as being useful to it. Sociological and socio-psychological research over the last twenty years has confirmed these insights.

The relative independence of the formal and informal orders does not mean that there are no connections or causal interactions between them. It simply means that both of these modes of organization can be varied relatively independently of one other. The style of their changes is different. Informal expectations change continuously, slowly, and imperceptibly, led by experiences and disappointments as well as by the approval or opposition of others. Their content, certainties, the strength of their norms, as well as their perceived consensus may alter. Their history, justifications, and connections with other expectations transform them into a variety of reinterpretations. By contrast, formal expectations are linked to clear-cut identities. They are either valid or they are not. So it is that formal modes of ordering do not adjust to their environment in a continuous manner, but through decisions – which is to say jerkily, with thresholds, between static interludes.

These variations in the style of change necessarily lead to differences and inconsistencies.[6] The informal mode of ordering cannot react immediately to the new boss in an appropriate manner – and so its first reaction is emotional. It takes time for it to find the certainty and consensus necessary for the formation of adequate expectations.

Installing someone in a formal position thus is not accompanied by succession to the informal functions of the predecessor. The boss's informal functions are usually practiced more or less latently and are anything but obvious to their successor. They may consist, for instance, in the boss continually mediating between different organizational cliques, and by doing so, avoiding open conflicts. They may also consist in the boss joining an exclusive group, so giving him access to confidential information that he can use to keep the organization under control. In other cases, the boss's good relationships with outsiders or with managers may well protect the organization. It is also possible that an extremely tolerant style of leadership that shies away from intervening has shaped expectations in the informal order.

In all such cases – and this is the gist of our analysis – the informal order cannot count on the continuation of a correspondingly informal allocation of functions. There is no stipulation that the succession from one boss to another will ensure the continuation of the interrelationship between formal and informal work in its entirety. It cannot even be expressed as a legitimate expectation, because the informal regime has no language for it. Since there is no institutional transition, a period of uncertainty prevails until the informal regime has adjusted, and until the informal functions associated with the old boss have been replaced and a new boss, with perhaps different functions, has been integrated into the organization.

These problems will be exacerbated by those language and communicative difficulties already mentioned. Faced with an unfamiliar person, especially an unfamiliar manager, only formally legitimated definitions of situations and expectations can be deployed. Anything else would be inappropriate, offensive to the accepted way of expressing oneself, and likely to result in embarrassing rebuffs.

On the one hand, such inhibitions of free expression provide a protective function for the formal organization. The coherence of its idealized self-presentation is not jeopardized. Moreover, they also include sensible role-separation mechanisms. One cannot, for example, induce the boss, nor be induced by the boss, to reveal information about off-duty matters.

On the other hand, the habitual societal forms and methods of getting to know one other wither under such circumstances. Admittedly, people always meet each other while performing specifically defined roles – perhaps as travel companions or fishermen, theatergoers or invited guests. However, these roles, unlike professional roles, contain no taboos against building on such acquaintance. People get to know each other through a process of careful revelations that permit those involved to determine their respective status and to establish those forms of self-presentation and understanding of the situation that may lead to a consensus within this particular relationship. Both sides raise their visors to the degree that there is a prospect of consensus,[7] and each gives the other tactful warnings when they are entering into dangerous territory. For such an interaction it is essential that one does not remain tied to the initial role in which one made the other's acquaintance, but instead explores other roles of one's conversation partner. In this way one learns whether he is a refugee, actively engaged in a war situation, the father of two children, a church leader, or an allotment gardener and a member of a fencing club. In fact, one needs to find out not only that he performs such roles, but also how he relates to them.

In summary, it can be said that structural ordering that operates within formal organizations, and in particular larger, differentiated systems, weighs down changes in leadership with problems. They are able to legitimize only part of the expectations that are necessary for effective functioning, and, therefore, are able to regulate leadership successions only to a limited degree. The change of leadership takes place abruptly and leaves any new distribution of informal functions wide open. Any relief of those tensions that would have followed this change of leadership, as well as any furtherance of mutual acquaintance, is delayed and obstructed by built-in barriers to communication.

## II

There is a strong tendency in daily life to attribute difficulties, problems, tensions, and disappointments to the characteristics and conduct of the people involved, and to explain them accordingly. It is someone's fault, because he is ambitious, selfish, lazy, or vain. Similarly, a person is considered incompetent because he does not fulfill certain expectations. Explanations such as these are in general quite adequate for daily use.

Frequently, however, individual behavior is merely a reaction to the system conditions under which it takes place. It constitutes an attempt to come to terms with the difficulties that have come about as the consequences of a particular type of social regime. Accordingly, social science directs its attention to those system stipulations that govern action – an approach already very prominent in Marx – and so provides new perspectives and different explanatory possibilities.

If one selects a social regime with a highly differentiated division of labor, one cannot avoid certain consequential problems. A feature that characterizes the disadvantages that flow from fundamental structural decisions is that these decisions cannot easily be counteracted; there is no magic bullet. If easy solutions were possible, they could be integrated in the structure of roles and the difficulties would disappear. The very least one can expect is that systemic consequences, which do not depend on the individual character of the people involved, re-occur in a recognizably typical way. For this reason, it must be possible to study them as such and to point out those aspects of a situation that heighten or relieve tension.

Without claiming that it is either complete or systematic, one can set out a list of the variables relevant to the situation of a change of boss.[8] These are: (1) the legitimacy of the change according to informal norms and value judgments; (2)

bureaucratic regulations concerning the position and the change; (3) the new boss's previous history either in or outside the organization; and (4) the personality of the predecessor.

1. The formal legitimacy of a change of position can generally be assumed. In addition to this, however, employees have their own ideas about the reasons justifying such a change.[9] The finest nuances and distinctions are discussed and elaborated upon. The criteria for gaining a position are not the same as for its loss. Firings, geographical transfers of personnel, redeployments to a different office in the same location, reassignments to different positions within the same office, and changes in the assignment of tasks and responsibilities are all judged according to different criteria. In public administration, for instance, actual, or suspected, political influence can create a problem. To be sure, someone's political appointment to a cabinet-level position is accepted as a matter of course. In the lower ranks, however, at least some visible professional qualifications are required as well as political ones, and, especially in the early stages, they are checked with particular zeal. The transfer of a civil servant for political reasons is frowned upon,

but this is not necessarily the case when a civil servant is simply entrusted with other tasks.

It is not possible to work this out in detail, due to a lack of empirical studies even in the American literature. In general, however, it can be said that the approval or disapproval associated with a change is easily transferred to the person of the successor. If the successor, from the moment he takes office, already thwarts the expectations of his new work environment, he can count on people's distrust.

Such distrust has a real basis. The reasons for change often impose a certain implicit direction on the successor, which may limit his sensitivity to local expectations and even instill in him a critical attitude. This is the case especially when the change is linked to criticism of the way in which the office had been previously carried out or with the expectation that a new, different course is about to be taken. The same applies when a successor owes his appointment to another person and now wants to meet that person's expectations. All of these circumstances tend to make the successor visibly skeptical about local practices and are, therefore, likely to arouse resistance.

2. In a general sense, bureaucratic regulations

relieve the tensions resulting from changes in personnel. Small private enterprises are hardest hit by problems of succession. The positions of their bosses are highly customized. They rest on specific combinations of experience, knowledge, and ability and, because of the narrow set-up within which they operate, they can be neither formalized nor reduced to abstract guiding principles. For this reason, the replacement of the boss in such cases is often equivalent to putting the survival of the company at risk.[10]

By contrast, in a full-blown bureaucracy – for instance, in public administration – every position, even the boss's, is staffed with mobility in mind. Here, the possibility of change is the basis of all relationships. Any type of equilibrium that relies on specific people is, in a certain way, always tentative and is also experienced and institutionalized as such. Thus, a change never comes entirely unexpectedly. At the very least, everyone has already experienced something like it and, therefore, holds in reserve predetermined ways of reacting for just such a case. Whenever bureaucratic regulation increases, the occasions for change, and the forms that change takes, as well as the consequences of change, become more predictable. At any rate, the permanent features associated with the position of boss, his duties, his powers, and his position according to the formal communication network, are known. This makes a good number of predictions possible. Furthermore, the formal regulation of behavior can deprive the informal regime of many of its functions and, in extreme cases, reduce it to mere participation in chat- and leisure-time-groups that remain indifferent toward the goings-on of the organization and instead only address and satisfy personal needs. Even the new boss has hardly any difficulties with such groups. No doubt, promising possibilities for relieving tension are to be found along these lines, as is noted by Grusky[11] and Gouldner.[12] There is, however, a significant trade-off, for these possibilities bring with them all the well-known disadvantages of formal bureaucracy.

3. A further aspect overlaps questions of legitimacy and the bureaucratization of change. This is whether the new boss has risen up from within the organization itself, or has come from the outside. Both solutions to the problem of succession have advantages and disadvantages.[13] There are good reasons for the old Prussian practice of not

recruiting the heads of government agencies from the agencies themselves. That said, we should not lose sight of both the drawbacks of this practice and considerations that speak in favor of recruiting internal talent.

Whoever comes from the outside is a stranger, and has to start his appointment in the role of a stranger. Those general characteristics of the role of strangers described by Simmel apply to him.[14] The stranger brings attitudes and expectations that were not formed under the social control of the group. He is relatively free, more objectively and abstractly oriented, and not bound by his own earlier decisions. For him, the entire situation is new, that is to say, unstructured. For the people who surround him, however, only a single element of their world changes. Typically, this results in different attitudes toward innovations that contain potential for conflict. Furthermore, the new boss may safely assume that all innovations are recorded as his own personal successes.[15] In other situations within the context of organized work, it is quite rare for it to be so clearly stated where the merit lies. As a result, the new boss will be prone to making changes. In any event, his initial role brings with it a freedom from and lack of respect for local practices. Such a mindset on his part is expected, and no matter how carefully he proceeds, those around him become skeptical and reserved. They are on the defensive.

Because he is a stranger, and also because of possible animosity toward him, his initial communications with others are limited to formally prescribed and professionally necessary situations and, in addition, perhaps to the attempts that others may make to gain favor with their new boss. Such communications are not very rich in content. Typically, the new boss does not receive the information necessary to control the informal regime. He only learns what he probably already knows or what comes his way through official channels, but not what is expected of him and what he can expect.[16]

Such withholding of communications that presuppose the existence of trust can lead to isolation, which exacerbates the uncertainty of expectations on both sides. So it was that in the US, after the Eisenhower administration moved in, there was talk of the "hostile native complex"[17] of the new boss. The successor always has the opportunity to govern by stressing and expanding his formal powers, insisting on the observance of general

rules and standing directives and breaking resistance by means of sanctions. Alternatively, he
can use the reassignment and new definition of
important posts as a way of creating an environment around him that he can trust and use to
help him gain control over the organization.

In cases when the new boss comes from within
the ranks of the organization, there is a different
situation with a different distribution of advantages and disadvantages. To begin with, the boss's
initial role is quite different, albeit not any less
difficult. The successor has already been included
in a network of individualized expectations. He
is already "socialized" and has a personal face. It
can be assumed that he knows what is expected
of him. He is familiar with local symbols and
the less-than-explicit background to a conversation. His favorite topics and prejudices are well
known, which makes talking to him easier. He
is not a stranger and therefore has sufficient
opportunities to inform himself. He can assert
his claims vis-à-vis others without having to use
his formal authority.

On the other hand, the new boss is subject to
claims based on past benefits, favors, and friend-
ship. He lacks the freedom provided by the role

of a stranger. He has to behave in accordance with his new position, and so he initially has to disappoint those expectations that rely on his old status. This change will be easier for him if he has already occupied a high rank in the informal regime and carried out informal leadership functions, which will mean that his appointment just amounts to ratifying an expected succession.

It has also been observed in the case of industrial administration in America, which relies to a high degree on internal talent, that the new boss often brings along his own clique. Not just a single person, but a whole group rises in status.[18] This provides decisive advantages – the new boss brings along his old management tool and at the same time strengthens his own personal standing within the group, which is indebted to him for its collective promotion. The costs of this solution usually consist in the intensification of tensions between cliques in the organization. Those who have been systematically overlooked become unhappy and sullen. When the next change in leadership takes place, there remains a group of old acolytes at the top, who have lost their place in the order of things and are not easily utilized. Presumably they organize resistance against the next boss.[19]

In public administration this attendant rise of the old cliques may well prove more difficult, since personnel decisions are more formalized. Yet here as well, there is a tendency in the case of internal appointments for the new boss to retain his old connections and govern with their support.

Obviously, these considerations do not allow for any general recommendations. Neither outside appointments nor internal ones ought to be preferred as a matter of principle.[20] Both solutions give rise to advantages and disadvantages, and their results cannot be compared. For these reasons, one cannot expect from a scientific analysis more than the mere differentiation of resulting problems. Moreover, even for practitioners, it may be more fruitful to find out which resulting problems they must keep under observation when choosing one of the possible solutions, rather than seeking the theoretically correct solution.

4. A further factor is the personality of the predecessor, the functions that he fulfilled, and his present whereabouts. A comparison between successor and predecessor becomes irresistible once one considers the character of the posi-

tion of "boss" within the organization, and this comparison gives the employees' expectations a particular note.

The transition is easier if a successor with similar attitudes and practices takes on the office, if he belongs to the same party, or if he underwent the same professional training or had a similar career to that of his predecessor. The transition becomes more difficult if the successor was selected for the post as a direct contrast to his predecessor, for instance when a professorial type follows a businessman or a lawyer replaces a party politician. In such cases, a corresponding contrast in behavior is to be expected and will be read into the situation. This by itself shifts the emphasis and the possibilities. Naturally, employees will seek to approach the boss in accordance with the behavior they expect of him. For the boss it is exceedingly difficult to escape such preemptive stereotyping. It is a slow process that succeeds only to the degree that the people in the organization get to know him personally and develop a sense of what can be expected from him as an individual.

What is more, one very frequently observes that such contrasts in the maintenance of expectations tend to be generalized. If the new boss is labeled as different, there is the expectation that he will decide differently from his predecessor in every case. This gives new hope to those who have previously been the underdogs. Old and previously hopeless requests are presented anew. Even the predecessor is pressed into this scheme and is reinterpreted in the contrasting context of the present problems. This leads to the posthumous reevaluation of former bosses, for which Gouldner coined the term, "Rebecca Myth."[21]

Besides, whether the old boss continues to be active on stage or behind the curtain is important.[22] This is rather obvious in cases where he continues to be employed by the same organization in a higher rank. Yet this is not the only case. For instance, if there has been a political change, the internal shift of power in government departments is absorbed to some extent when former bosses remain active as deputies. This element is lacking in the political power play of the United States. This may be one of the reasons for the wide-ranging personnel and administrative repercussions that a political change at the presidential level brings with it.

# III

In addition to those already discussed, there is certainly an array of other factors. There are, for instance, the homogeneity or divisiveness of attitudes in the organization, the strength and direction of its members' interest in participating – especially the degree to which indifference or, alternatively, aggressive jockeying for influence predominates – what kind of leadership the organization needs, the threat to the organization from external forces, and the extent that routine plays in its decisions.

Instead of extending our investigation in these directions and in the process compartmentalizing the problem even further, let us try to gain a unified perspective. At issue was the observation that in large formal organizations, oriented around a specific purpose, the change of leadership roles is only partially institutionalized and therefore necessarily leaves many problems open, uproots expectations, creates uncertainties, and brings about the need to stabilize new alignments.

In all of this, there is little danger that the disorder will be a lasting one, even if it may chronically re-occur. There will always be new expectations, adjusted to the situation, that in time will settle down. The problem is not so much one of adaptation costs or diminished performance during a time of transition. Rather, there is a real danger that new expectations will be established that are not in line with the aims of the formal organization and do not support its leadership structure. Instead a self-directed, informal organization – consisting of cliques of old insiders – may split off, as a specific consequence of the change in leadership. It may exclude the boss, spin a cocoon around him, and reduce him to his formal responsibilities. Under these conditions, subordinates perform their own, perfectly idealized, show on the theme of careful, diligent, overworked employees and their manager is treated as its audience.[23] All facts that contradict this performance are kept from the manager so that he will be unable to find any starting point for objective criticism, and any doubt concerning the employees' self-presentation will appear as tactless and in bad taste.

Despite having a plethora of contacts through his high status, the manager becomes communicatively isolated. The information he receives is filtered. His decisions move along paths of predetermined alternatives. His organization's flaws are pointed out to him by people from outside. If he probes a bit deeper, he is met with premeditated explanations and justifications. He remains the prominent star, because this role is fixed by the formal organization, but his performance is decided by others. His high status is put to use for the ratification of decisions, for ceremonial purposes, for legitimizing problematic practices, and for the transformation of the system's requirements into demands that are directed outward to the system's environment.

This kind of ordering can undoubtedly be considered a solution to the stabilization problem created by a change of leadership. It may work quite satisfactorily. The traditional view of organizations as formal authority hierarchies did not really give this possibility the attention and recognition it deserves. Whereas the art of leading subordinates has been discussed for centuries and there have been theories, systems, experiments, courses, and an unmanageable wealth of literature on the topic, the art of steering managers has until now attracted little attention, despite the fact that in many cases it may well be more important for the stability of a social system.

Even those who are free from prejudices and impartially recognize the merits of such an arrangement still need to face up to certain of its disadvantages. These are especially noticeable with regard to the organization's external relationships. In such cases, the way in which influence actually works deviates considerably from what is presented on the formal organizational chart. Outsiders are not familiar with this internal distribution of power and so have to rely on the formal version of how the organization operates. For this reason, they do not gain access to the most efficient communication channels. The organization, in turn, faces adaptation difficulties, because it no longer meets the expectations of its environment. It therefore raises the question of what alternatives and what equivalent solutions to the problem are available.

There is another possibility, which we have already encountered earlier. It consists of increasing the bureaucratization and formalization of all measures.[24] The new boss may try to govern primarily through the means made available by the formal organization. These consist of creating a tight network of general rules applying to all cases, installing reliable checks, and punishing their violation. Within such a framework, subordinates are treated individually, regardless of their informal relations with one another, for only individuals can be held responsible. Whenever this is possible, the informal order, with all its instinctive ties, its support network, its granting and accepting of favors, its information, its reciprocal claims, its personal obligations, and its emotional security, will be reduced.

Measures such as these correspond to the ideal type of impersonal, bureaucratic administration depicted by Max Weber. To be sure, such a style of leadership may well be feasible in smaller units with correspondingly limited tasks. It cannot simply be dismissed as misguided, as the American literature on the subject tends to do nowadays.

More recent organizational research has, however, led to doubts as to whether large organizations can in fact be successfully governed in this way. The assumption that large organizations specifically ought to be managed in a formal bureaucratic manner needs to be reassessed, at least where senior management is concerned. A number of the most recent research findings may well evoke an interest in a more generalized manner of system steering. Among these findings are problems concerning managers' work overload; the inevitability of contradictory performance standards; the shortcomings of classical organizational science and its association with the means–ends schema and the command model of authority; and the advantages of a personally oriented "natural" action system in which behavior is steered by tact, trust, the exchange of favors, differences in prestige, and subtler forms of social sanction.

In this context, besides the techniques of monetary steering, the expansion of the boss's personal relationships with a limited circle of subordinates deserves special attention. It is true that the initial optimism of the "human relations" movement has given way to increased skepticism. Moreover, it could not be confirmed in general terms that special consideration for personal human concerns fosters the formal purposes of an organization, and attempts to increase professional motivation by such means have not been particularly successful.[25] Perhaps, however, the way the question was framed in this first wave of observations and experiments was still too much dominated by the traditional theory of formal, purpose-specific organizations and by the problem of inadequate work motivation. It is unfeasible to expect good treatment to replace lack of enthusiasm for one's work.

There is another, separate question – namely, whether it is in fact necessary for effective leadership in large systems for the boss to assume certain functions in the informal work regime of his subordinates. Is it possible for him to recognize the problems that plainly dominate everyday work? Is it possible for him to be able to find his way through the intrigues, claims, and exchanges that are instrumental in the distribution and allocation of promotions, responsibilities, and access to sources of information, or for him to be able to understand the significance of making use of offenses against and deviations from the norm? Is it possible for him to be well versed in informal status symbols and the different forms of prestige and for him to learn to influence this entire system? Because of his formal status, the manager is inevitably a key figure in this system. The only question is whether he is being used – against his will and knowledge – or whether he has mastered the system.

Up till now, behavioral arrangements of this

kind have been overshadowed by the formal organization's monopoly of legitimacy. Research into them has only just started. It would be premature, therefore, to pass judgment or make recommendations. Nonetheless, there are many indications of a convergence between the two main trends that determine organization science today – sociological and socio-psychological research into actual behavior and the theory of the rational control of systems. In our context this means that a status based on informal functions and performance within the informal regime makes the leading of large organizations easier, and opens up possibilities for reliable delegation and selective information – in short, possibilities for generalized system control that are not available to a manager who acts in a purely formal capacity.

# The Spontaneous Creation of Order

## Man in Administration

*The world of work: social and emotional priva-tions.* Every organization consists of actions. Yet nobody can act without himself being present. He brings himself, his personality, along to work. The organization, however, requires only par-ticular forms of behavior from him. His feelings and interest in self-expression are barely touched upon in this process. During work they loiter functionless, and cause damage if they are not kept under control.

Work as such is organized rationally. Its con-sistency, however, is not the inner consistency of private life. For this reason, what a worker would like to accomplish often remains unheard, while expressions of his innermost being remain unseen. The worker comes to regard the cool indifference toward him as a unique being as a lack of opportunity and fulfillment. Under the keyword "alienation" one finds a vast literature within critical sociology that searches for symptoms of social and emotional deprivations in work organizations. True, more recent empirical research concerning job satisfaction paints a more agreeable picture overall than might have been expected, but it cannot be denied that habituation plays a role in this context and that many are content only because they own a television set and do not hope for anything better.

*Individual versus organization?* Theory loves contrasts. From the start, therefore, it assumed a direct opposition between individuals and organizations. This seems to throw some light on our dilemma. Influential trends in the intellectual history of the nineteenth century, especially its preference for the dialectic of simple concepts and its fascination with industrial conflict, supported and solidified this conceptual scheme.

Yet the heat of the quarrel between individualism and collectivism caused this formulation of the problem to evaporate. The onset of empirical social research also contributed to the increasing need for more careful and more differentiated ideas. Moreover, the more that research, which had started in production companies, began to encroach upon management companies, the more it became absolutely clear that a rigid theory of conflict would not do. For such a theory cannot give a sufficient account of either the elasticity of the organization or the plasticity of human attitudes.

*The humanization of the organization.* First of all came the call to change the organization. Today, it is widely accused of applying the "classical" organization model. In the motivational theory of classical organizational science, it was assumed that people were free to choose and in this sense were understood as rational beings. The underlying belief had been that people could be motivated to perform the prescribed work, if their own, indigenous motives were supplemented by alien ones that contradicted the behavior that they personally desired, so dragging people away from the course of action that seemed natural. The new theory was a success, although this success depended mainly on the strength of the new conflicting motives and on their proximity to actual behavior. Shrewd systems of wage payments and strict supervision were helpful in achieving these objectives.

What this approach could not see was the conflict itself. The classical theory of motivation implies mastery over people through implanting conflict within the person. It was only when the more recent, empirical, behavioral sciences paid more attention to actual people that it became recognized that this conflict creates too much stress. For this very reason, all of the more recent endeavors are directed toward relieving tensions. Nowadays, psychology and psychiatry, as well as anthropology, social psychology, and sociology, conceive of people as highly complex action systems that are guided through self-consciousness and anxiety and whose conscious and unconscious functional conditions require serious consideration on the part of the organization.

The new humaneness of the organization exists in its better technical adjustment to the human condition, not in a weakening of the organization's objectives or its principle of rationality. It was expected that the organization would adjust its structural decisions to people's limited rational capacities, so as not to overtax them; that it would provide, or at least tolerate sympathetically, compensatory benefits, such as frequent and friendly exchanges between employees; and that it would create a humane "work climate" through a correspondingly humane leadership ideology – a climate in which all can thrive and so work all the harder.

*Administrators' adaptation strategies.* Whereas suggestions for the cultivation of "human relations" were developed with production organizations in mind, it seems that the current, still sparse, research on individuals' adaptation strategies is likely to gain more valuable knowledge from the study of administrative bureaucracies. After all, those in administrations are predestined to become tacticians.

Administrations are, according to the real meaning of the term, enterprises for the production of binding decisions. Both the actions that take place internally and those directed at the outside world consist essentially of communications. To be sure, communications offer people better opportunities for self-presentation and self-assertion than strictly manual operations, the meaning of which is revealed at the end of the assembly line as an enormous quantity of identical products. It is not (yet) possible to program and specialize communications in such a way that their production could dispense with the human individual's memory and skills in bringing things together. For this reason, even where communications have to be presented as factual statements, they are also still attributed to people.

Consequently, the human dilemma in industrial organization does not occur with the same urgency in administration. This is as true for public administration as it is for administration in industry and social organizations. Especially in the upper echelons and among the higher offices, there are more opportunities for the administrator's personality to make an appearance and so also more incentives for him to adjust his personality to the requirements of a successful self-presentation within the system. He can, for instance, demonstrate the adroitness of his routines or stress the impersonal quality of his actions in order to make it appear that he, himself, becomes visible only after the end of the working day. For example, he may choose the path of gaining status and rising in the hierarchy. He may aim at being personally "irreplaceable" for the performance of certain services, or he may, as it were, produce his wine from the offshoots of great projects, so that his role as instigator will be recognized by those in the know. His own prospects do not lose their relevance, but they are structured by the organization in such a way that he has to perform only a minimal number of formal duties to achieve his personal goals.

*Rationalization and self-discipline.* Although the rationality of the organization and the inner logic of a person's private world follow entirely different, unconnected system laws, there exists nonetheless – perhaps precisely because of this – a certain margin for mutual adjustment. This margin can be widened by means of increased awareness and a strategic understanding of the interplay of both sides. If from time to time organizations critically examine their principles and human beings do the same with their feelings, it may be possible to discover more abstract behavioral premises and novel behavioral alternatives that make mutual adjustment easier.

It is not improbable that something like this

could happen. Comparing the administration of highly developed industrial states with that of developing countries makes it apparent that the most significant difference between them lies in the degree of personal immersion in an externally determined work role. It also lies in the degree to which an individual's personal environment, especially his family, recognizes the adjustments that are necessary for these purposes and attaches normative expectations to them. "Progress," then, consists in the institutionalization of those virtues that permit a personally acceptable existence without unnecessarily blocking out the organized system's own rationality. Examples of such virtues are as follows: wariness as to how one expresses oneself, and tact; a wide time horizon; a feeling for the far-reaching, complex, and indirect consequences of one's own actions and those of others; the evaluation of all events in terms of power, status implications, establishing precedents, opportunities for consensus, and gains by means of indirect paths; the ability to wait, and in particular the capacity to suspend one's own feelings and need for self-presentation until the right moment; the ability to tolerate and relieve tensions; and the inner preparedness for accepting second-best solutions and for recognizing the facts as they are, especially when they have already been decided upon. Finally, what underlies all this as its presupposition is self-discipline. Incidentally, the "modernization" of citizenship in developing countries follows this same trajectory.

## The Myth of the Small Group

*The discovery of "informal organization."* Our portrayal of the integration of the person into an organization finds many points of reference in the more recent organizational sciences. Yet it is not representative of the full scope of this work. Many theories and research projects are based on the discovery of an "informal organization" or "informal groups" within the firm. This discovery was the result of a series of extensive experiments that were conducted from 1927 to 1932 by the Harvard Business School at the Hawthorne facilities of the Western Electric Company. Their analysis had enormous influence on the subsequent development of the sociology of firms and administration.

Briefly summarized, the findings from these studies reveal that, besides the official, prescribed organization, there exists another social regime that provides its own norms and institutions. Thus, autonomous leadership roles and informal sanctions make their appearance. There exist particular, preferred topics of communication, particular, reciprocal points of view, and a sort of emotional logic, clarifying the work situation, its operational factors, and its dangers. All of these satisfy the common interests of those who work together and articulate, socially manage, and defend these interests against the management.

*Scientific output.* These new insights destroyed the prevailing formula of an antithesis between the individual and the collective, on which the older organizational science had based a reward/sanction theory of motivation. It now became clear that the work organization could not be equated with the social system and that, in turn, an individual's recalcitrant behavior within the enterprise did not arise exclusively from individual motives, but was rather, to some extent at least, socially codetermined. As a consequence, sociology was able to leave organizational objectives and the means for their optimum realization to management science and instead concentrate on the newly discovered, separate field of informal organization – a division of labor that persists today.

The first theoretical expression of all of this could be found in the concept of the group. It seemed that this concept could explain all those informal manifestations that could not be derived from the organization's objective, and was able to link them to familiar general phenomena. Following this initial insight, but moving far beyond it, a comprehensive field of research dedicated to small groups developed in the United States. It includes a wide array of investigations, which is only loosely connected with organizational science, ranging from socio-psychological experiments through sociological models of role assignments all the way to the construction of variables that can be put in mathematical terms.

*Socio-political hopes.* The fertility of research into groups can hardly be challenged, given the skepticism of current judgments on the general socio-political hopes that the leader of the Hawthorne experiments, Elton Mayo, and some of his disciples and successors had placed in the nature of groups. Mayo thought that he had struck gold in the subterranean spontaneity of informal groups and hoped to reinvigorate industry's sagging work morale. If only industry itself were to pay attention to this phenomenon and adjust its organization accordingly, so as to nourish and cherish emotionally stabilized groups, these groups might become the seeds of a restoration to a healthy society.

One basic idea within this conception is undoubtedly correct – namely, that groups are easier to influence than individuals with their complicated and, at the same time, hardened psychic constitutions. Also productive were those impulses toward a "humanizing" of organizations that were brought into play. In all remaining respects, the far-reaching optimism, which had certain parallels in the continental European professional guild movement, has faded away.

*Small groups and large organizations.* The analogy of work group and intimate group does not go very far. In large labor organizations special conditions for forming groups prevail. They are structurally determined and cannot be changed, unless one wishes to turn the organization into a company for the promotion of "the good life" among select friends. If this alternative is barred, the following question emerges: under what circumstances is it at all possible for emotionally stabilized groups to form and survive in a rationally structured world of work that imposes precisely defined behavioral demands – except perhaps in organizing resistance?

Ever since William Foote Whyte's groundbreaking article,[1] this weakness in group theory has been generally acknowledged. There is less awareness of how deep this weakness goes. The reason that it so far remains uncorrected lies in the group concept itself. Traditionally, it designates a purely internal order. Up to now, neither group theory nor group experiments have paid enough attention to the groups' adaptation to a difficult environment. In cases where informal groups exist, large organizations are their environment. The question of the conditions that result in a group choosing a form of adaptation to its environment that is either agonistic to, or oriented by, particular aims has so far barely been raised, let alone answered.

*The special situation of administration.* In addition to all these objections, there is also the extreme uncertainty regarding the extent to which true informal groups that are worthy of the name actually take shape. In any case, it seems that as a result of the stronger, hierarchical structuring in administrative organizations, the group entity here appears to be much more complicated, and far less consolidated, than some of the findings of American industrial sociology suggest. We shall return to this point.

Apart from that, skepticism regarding the group phenomenon and its factual reach ought not to mislead us into underestimating the significance of informal aspects of behavior, even, and in fact especially, in administrations. Although making binding decisions is always formally programmed, and this is the real task of administration, in public administration at least, formal (professionally accountable) and informal (spontaneous, provisional, indirect) communications run side by side in all preparations for decision-making.

From the results of the research done in industrial sociology at least, one finding can be applied to administration: Those formal behavioral expectations that have to be heeded by everyone who would like to continue their membership of the system do not amount to the complete picture. They do not convey the full reality of actual behavior. Moreover, taken in isolation, they cannot survive, if they are not supplemented by spontaneous, yet socially ordered, behavior that fulfills complementary functions.[2]

## Spontaneity and its Social Conditions

*Spontaneous, factually oriented action.* In the more recent organizational science, the words "informal" and "spontaneous" are often used synonymously, and not much effort is made to explain the concept of spontaneity. This is unfortunate, especially because the traditional meaning of this concept, as refined in philosophy and psychology, makes it unusable for our purposes. According to the traditional understanding, an action is spontaneous if its cause can be found in itself. It is precisely this notion of purely individually attributable action, however, which has been surpassed by the discovery of the "informal organization."

More recent social psychology and sociology put at our disposal the means to reshape this notion of spontaneity, provided that we focus not on the causes of actions, but on the underlying degree of reflection. People act spontaneously precisely to the degree that they orient themselves exclusively according to the meaning of their actions in a certain situation, and do not concern themselves with whether others agree with them or with the impression they may make on others. Spontaneous action is factually oriented action whose social impact has not been considered. It can unfold only in situations in which consensus is ensured, in which trust in being correctly understood exists, and in which any special precautions and considerations can be dispensed with, because there is no danger of embarrassing oneself. For these reasons, spontaneous action can thrive only if certain social preconditions have been fulfilled. A separate science – sociometry – has established itself for the purpose of investigating these preconditions.

So-called spontaneous action is limited by the particular social framework that the structural decisions of an organized administration bring with them. The two most important features of this framework are the specification and regulation of the obligation to achieve consensus and the enduring character of interpersonal relationships.

*Limited and regulated consensus.* Unlike in families or circles of friends, there is no expectation in administrations that a consensus has to be reached on more or less any topic. Rather, there is a precise regulation of what an employee must acknowledge, and of what procedures exist for formulating the views with which everyone has to agree. The certainty that, within the range of topics covered by such a framework, there will always be a decision respected by everyone, in combination with the predictability of the entire decision-making process, facilitates a high degree of spontaneity in day-to-day formal and informal collaboration. No one has to fear that his or her partners will suddenly bare their teeth, make inappropriate jokes, or express unreasonable personal desires that it would be embarrassing to reject. The institutional framing of interpersonal contact protects everyone from such surprises. The price to pay for such protection is, however, that the law of role specification also applies to oneself. As a result, one has to suppress one's own capricious ideas and can no longer present naïvely and unrestrainedly just how one feels.

Under such conditions, spontaneity becomes role-specific and thus constrained. In the process, it loses much of its originality and credibility, for it is certainly possible to act in a dutiful, relevant way, but it is not so easy to act in a dutiful, spontaneous way. In administration, there is, rightly or not, a widespread suspicion of unacknowledged, hidden assumptions and ulterior motives.

*The mandatory continuation of contacts.* Perhaps even more important is the modification of natural spontaneity through the lasting nature of contacts. In intimate groups, endurance strengthens the relationship. In administrations, where participants, through their membership, work together in specific roles, the fact that continuing contacts are not motivated by their agreeable nature creates a problem. You have to work together if you want to remain members of the organization, and you will encounter the same people again under different circumstances and again where dependencies may vary. The law of re-encounter prevails. It is therefore appropriate both to exercise caution, and to reflect on anything that might have the potential to damage the relationship.

Nevertheless, trusting and relatively candid interaction based on positive personal acquaintance is possible, but not without the background awareness that you will have to work together even in the absence of such a good understanding. The institutional framework guarantees that even opponents have to cooperate. At the same time, it also undoes the spontaneity that would motivate cooperation between friends.

*The style of expression for administrative actions.* The social frameworks for spontaneity are also evident in the style in which administrative actions are expressed. Such measures are first and foremost serious actions – all the way into their underlying, concealed motives. They present themselves as linked to specific tasks and to subjects awaiting immediate decision-making. They also appear as circumspect and discreet, and at the same time as offering suggestions – as spontaneously interested, yet also reflective. Both bias and impartiality are avoided in equal measure. Moreover, administrative actions present themselves as fully verbalizable, although everyone knows that unspoken motives also play their part. For all those reasons, these actions invariably foster distrust, on the one hand. Yet, on the other hand, the sharing of this measured style by all members of an administration leads to a sort of commitment to which novices will quickly grow accustomed. This makes it possible for extremely complicated tasks of information-processing to be assigned to an administration without having to take into account either the interests or the individual traits of the actors involved, or their usual ways of expressing themselves.

## Collegiality

*The fulfillment of tasks and the representation of the system.* Reflective spontaneity is not only evident in the style in which communications are expressed. It also forms the structure for numerous ancillary institutions that make possible and facilitate collaboration in administrations and yet cannot be legitimated directly as the means to an end.

The fulfillment of tasks is altogether another matter. Here, one can always put in a request, within certain limits, for essential resources – for more paper, personnel, or money. In addition, however, there are particular collaboration problems that cannot be identified and solved in this official way. The tasks undertaken by an administration form its legitimate, external side. Yet they contain only a one-sided selection of expectations and facts and do not present the complete reality of concrete experience and action. Like all external interactions, they are stylized. Even their presentation requires measures that cannot be openly revealed; for instance, all the efforts that have to be spent on making communications convincing, the hiding of weaknesses and mistakes, or overcoming internal differences of opinion. An English observer quite accurately characterized the formulation of replies to parliamentary questions as "supreme instances of art concealing itself. If they were publicly recognized as masterpieces they would not be so."[3]

In order to have control over the external view, you need an internal view that provides the perspective for decisions on what may and what must not become visible. The keepers of this difference between the external and internal views are the community of colleagues. Even if they do not know each other well, colleagues expect a certain dedication and way of behaving that demonstrate an understanding of, and takes into account the difference between, internal and external. This approach constitutes the basic law of internal cooperation and is institutionalized as such. It does not presuppose the formation of a group.

*Facilitation of and barriers to communication.* The most important commandment for collegial cooperation concerns the regulation of language. "Thou shalt filter communications that are outwardly directed, or those that could get out of control." Written bureaucratic language makes official messages reliable and accountable. Internally, a freer mode of expression, which may be used to talk about the production of such communications, is allowed. This mode permits swift, practical, and comprehensive mutual understanding before the formal decision is made, and so constitutes an essential element in rational, highly skilled decision-making, although – or rather, because – not everything that is said can also be written down. In such cases, written memos serve merely to ratify the result that has already been reached and to keep the files in order.

Such linguistic discrepancy may strike unsympathetic observers as doublespeak. As a matter of fact, it assumes the existence of collegial trust – trust in the willingness and the ability of colleagues to respect the communication barriers that are in place. Loyalty, discretion, and a discreet mode of expression are institutionalized as collegial expectations. Those who are not able or willing to hold to them are put on the meager diet of purely formal and entirely harmless information, which considerably limits their ability to act and their potential influence.

*Equality as an issue of rank.* An undersupply of information is often the fate of the superior, who is at best a semi-colleague. His loyalty and discretion are hard to secure through purely collegial means, and his far-reaching communications are hard to control. This is why restraint seems appropriate in interactions with him – especially when he greets subordinates using an unusual form of salutation, such as "My dear chap," in order to signal inequality by stressing equality. Skillful superiors are at least capable of playing the role of manager and colleague side by side according to the situation, although they cannot play both roles at the same time. They have their accessible hours during which their existence as manager enters, as it were, a latent phase and candid talk, as if among colleagues, becomes possible.

Equality of rank is an essential element of the collegial style. It should not be mistaken for indifference to issues of hierarchy and rank, which nobody within a hierarchical structure can treat with impunity. Equality is the most sensitive of all the rank-based relationships and, therefore, it needs particularly careful protection. The unambiguousness of the official ranking associated with the hierarchical order makes it easier for colleagues of the same rank to recognize one another and treat each other appropriately. Conversely, the institutionalization of collegial equality protects the formal hierarchy against any competition that does not follow its rules. Whoever wants to win preference over his colleagues needs constantly to be striving after promotion and not just specific accomplishments.

*Maintenance of self-esteem.* Taking into account equality among colleagues and a certain shielding of collegial relationships against external scrutiny, probably the best way of finding out the criteria for esteem and self-esteem is to look for them among a circle of colleagues. Here, one does not compare oneself with either superiors or subordinates, who, on account of their different rank, occupy a different sphere. After all, the significance of the distinctions based on rank consists in relieving one from direct competition with those who are one's superiors. The pattern for determining the level of one's own aspirations is provided by the abilities and achievements of one's colleagues. Therefore, the esteem of colleagues and the exchange of tokens of mutual esteem are the most solid basis for maintaining and actually increasing self-esteem.[4]

A certain danger for the collegial conferring of esteem arises from the fact that in practical terms the superior's esteem is infinitely more important than that of individual colleagues. Employees who are aware that they are well regarded by their superiors are tempted to make their absence of dependence on their colleagues' esteem all too obvious. To guard against such an eventuality, good manners are important, and in addition a professional ethos that prevents colleagues from competing too aggressively for the patronage of their direct superior.

## The Segregation of Small Groups

*Work contacts.* Those components of collegial behavior that we have discussed – namely loyalty, a discreet mode of expression, and, within these parameters, communicative openness, the safeguarding of equality, mutual respect, and the curbing of competition by means of a professional ethos – are all elements of a general role that is directly related to problems that arise in organized collaboration. They do not come from the specific objective of an organization. Nevertheless, the institutionalization of the role of "the colleague" does not make up the whole of this spontaneous creation of order.

At the same time, daily collaboration creates social relations of a particular kind. It is in this context that the law of re-encounter, which we have already discussed, acquires its power. Every human contact requires a certain self-presentation by those involved. Their actions, statements, and decisions inevitably reveal something about themselves. Thus, they commit themselves to particular views or standards in front of partners who have a memory. In this way, repeated contacts over time consolidate social relationships that are linked to expectations of continuity. These relationships constitute small systems with their own norms. First and foremost among them is the requirement to stay true to the way in which one has presented oneself.

Contact systems condense the rather general relation of good collegiality into more intimate work relationships. The participants know each other personally. They can communicate swiftly while avoiding personal sensitivities or touchy subjects from the past. They can invoke by mere hints the complicated background of the subject matter on which work is to be done. They can trust in each other's ability to understand correctly constructive, well-meaning criticism. Such relationships are of high value since they make life and work easier, even if they do not usually either result in warmth of feeling or touch intimate areas of being. One can expect that a certain effort will be put into maintaining them and that, out of consideration for the good relationship, one's partners will act slightly differently than they would strictly have done, given the matter in hand. Included in this are such things as providing cover for each other, exchanging news, and a shared resistance to menacing innovations.

*Personal relationships.* Personal relationships may outlast work contacts, for example when such contacts are forcibly ended through transfers and promotions. Often their basis lies entirely outside the administration – for instance, in having shared time together at school, being members of the same college fraternity, common experiences as prisoners of war, a passion for tennis, or perhaps simply the fact that their gardens border one another.

Connections that reach beyond the daily, close-knit world of work have a similar character to, but serve an entirely different function from, that of good work relationships. Their meaning lies not in everyday routines, but in the out-of-the-ordinary. They serve as conduits that bypass the formally prescribed channels of communication – especially the official channels – by creating, as it were, the possibility of touching and moving the chess pieces in unauthorized ways.

Such short circuits have the air of something

illegal, since they cannot be elevated and turned into a universal law. It cannot be denied, however, that by these means much can be done in emergencies and urgent cases in ways that act as a corrective to all-too-sluggish, official procedures. For this reason, employees who are well connected are often considered real assets for those around them, especially if their connections reach all the way to the top or into the political sphere. Such rare employees cannot be forced, however, to use their connections in the service of a cause. They are in a position, therefore, to make demands in exchange for their willingness to help. At the very least, they will expect the particular esteem or gratitude of those around them.

*Organized work groups and cliques.* An individual's personal expressive style, generally observed collegiality, and good work contacts and relationships contribute bit by bit to the consolidation of spontaneous reactions in response to the behavioral conditions that are imposed on people in administrations. An even higher degree of consolidation is achieved through the creation of groups that comprise only a section of the members of an administration, combining them into a unit, and thus distinguishing them from the remainder. Whether they are in favor of or opposed to the objective of the official organization, the creation of such "informal organizations" does not have a uniform effect. These groups, rather, support contradictory tendencies.

Understanding the nature of groups is made easier if one distinguishes between organized work groups and cliques. Every administration is divided. It creates smaller units. There are departments, departmental sub-groups, and larger comprehensive units, whose members belong together by virtue of being members of the formal organization. In contrast, cliques are freer, bolder formations. They detach themselves from the little squares in the organizational chart and synthesize people from the most diverse work spheres and ranks into a community of common interest. Fixed cliques are relatively rare. Usually, one finds signs of true social cohesion and exaggerated fears only in the fantasies of their opponents.

*Focal issues of clique formation: dissatisfaction and tactics.* Because cliques do not have the structural support of formal organization at their disposal, other motives must justify their coming together. Such motives are not chosen randomly. Rather, they are tightly connected to the problems that come as consequences of formal organization.

Cliques tend to cluster around the dangers and opportunities of organized social coexistence. In administrations, there are two needs that dominate the formation of cliques. On the one hand, there is the need to express dissatisfaction, and, on the other, the need to further the interests of clique members by the use of strategies. Dissatisfied and strategic cliques can be distinguished from one another according to which of these needs is emphasized by the clique.

By means of a sophisticated sort of gossip, dissatisfied cliques work through the negative impressions and personal disappointments of life in an administrative organization. Their members are continuously adding new material and, above all, consensus. In this way, those who do not get promoted can nevertheless survive in more closely knit circles and can get rid of their frustration in a relatively innocuous way.

Whereas dissatisfied cliques outwardly display barely any ambition or liking for combat, strategic cliques are held together by the active pursuit of mutual interests, especially the exchange of useful information and the exploitation of personal relations. They place great value on the prominence and negotiating skills of their members and possess a certain inner structure that in some cases makes it possible for them to be treated as a unit in negotiations with their leaders.

## The Beginnings of a Distinct Group Organization

*The consciousness of belonging and membership fluctuations.* In the long term, our theory will probably do well to replace the concept of the group with the concept of the contact system. This has the additional advantage of being able to capture the notion of personal relationships, even for situations such as conferences, inspection rounds, and ceremonial occasions. It can capture their spontaneous, inherent laws and the particular conditions associated with success and failure. Nevertheless, groups in the narrow sense are a phenomenon all on their own. Their special feature is that in daily life they become conscious as social units. This conscious orientation by means of groups comes about in two stages. In the first place, some people are counted as members of a group, and others are not. Secondly, the group remains in existence, even when its members gradually change.

Groups in administration meet these conditions only partly and to differing degrees. Because of their formal organization, work groups possess clear criteria for membership and their continued existence is guaranteed despite their changing membership. They are groups in the most complete sense of the term. All the same, they are unable themselves to rule on their own membership. Their ability, therefore, to establish and enforce norms is severely limited. It is rare that cliques achieve a fully valid group consciousness that is separate from the orientation toward actual individuals. They possess no name. Their boundaries are not sharply defined. One immediately thinks of particular members when the clique is the focus of attention. In other cases, the nature and extent of cliques' participation is uncertain. In some situations, they are counted as belonging, but not in others. Moreover, a clique rarely survives the loss of its most prominent and active members. Newcomers may change the character of a clique to such an extent that it can no longer be seen as the same.

*The establishment of norms.* All members of an administration have to respect, if not follow, official norms. To do otherwise would put their membership at risk. In contact systems of all sorts, especially in work groups and cliques, there are additional, spontaneously created norms that regulate what can be expected of one another with respect to areas of behavior that are not formally fixed. These include:

- norms concerning the appropriate tone to be used;
- norms regarding mutual help and their limits;
- norms against boasting and showing off;
- norms against betraying specific secrets;
- norms against too much and too little work;
- norms that determine the thresholds one may negotiate up to in an informal and non-binding way;
- norms that indicate when and how one may warn another member of potential mistakes and threats;

- norms that regulate when one has to "take note" of unpleasant facts;
- norms that state whether and to what degree one may without question correct someone else's drafts;
- additional norms that regulate even the smallest details of working together.

By means of a sort of overriding, informal law these norms are backed up by formal ordering. This overriding law states that you should not blame anybody for trying formally to protect his own behavior.

Such spontaneously created norms can be found in every administration. Their validity, however, is limited by the fact that the officially validated norms claim a monopoly on legitimacy. The informal norms cannot be written down. Worse still, the groups that produce them have no control over membership within the system, so that they are unable effectively to remove from their work space anyone who scorns and boycotts their norms, just as long as the offender does not commit any breach of the formal rules. These groups may withdraw collegial support and the advantages of membership of the clique from offenders, but that is of little use if these offenders are capable people in secure positions.

*Prominence and leadership.* As in the case of normative behavioral expectations, the difference that exists between spontaneous justifications and those that rely on official decisions, that is to say, between informal and formal validity, also exists in issues of rank. The official pecking order based on rank is structured by the hierarchy of posts. Everyone has their assigned place that can only be changed by an explicit decision. In administration as in all interpersonal relationships, however, an additional rudimentary game of rank is also being played out. It carves an abundance of finely nuanced intermediate ranks into the few clear steps of the hierarchy.

Rudimentary rank is achieved in the struggle for control over a specific situation. Some people end up at the center of the situation because of their talent, the circumstances, their family background, or sheer coincidence. They become the center of attention in the eyes all other participants, and are in a position to define the character of the situation and to assign implicit roles to other participants. During longer collaborations, rank gradients of this sort become socially visible and will be expected by all participants. Under such circumstances, groups tend to assign to such prominent rank-bearers the functions of informal leadership and decision-making. In the process, they are presented with a role that consolidates their rank.

Not that they always get their own way. Typically, they lack the recognized, decision-making authority of a monarch. Unlike in formal organizations, authority and obedience are not fixed in terms of membership requirements. All the time there are specific situations where people at the margins are in a position to act as crowd-pullers because they possess certain information or know the right people. Collegial equality naturally also poses an obstacle to the concentration of power in the hands of informal leaders. Finally, since administrations offer multifarious opportunities for promotion, often a person's conspicuous, informal standing is very quickly formally recognized, which allows him to reenter the hierarchy at a higher level. Administrations, unlike production organizations, where these aspects are much less important, have little lasting informal leadership; rather, group leadership is often based on formal rank.

*Care in the group's external relations.* Among those topics relating to the spontaneous creation of norms, the issue of care in external relations between groups deserves special attention. We have already discussed a comparable rule of good collegiality in relation to the external boundaries of an administration. We now find the same problem situated along the internal boundaries.

Work groups and cliques also have problems here in making statements about themselves, particularly in those areas where they have to deviate from formal norms in order to make their life bearable. In such cases, it all comes down to using a special filter to conduct communications with not especially trustworthy colleagues or with superiors.

In most cases, these internal communication filters are usually contested, because they prevent an unqualified exchange of ideas prior to the official decision. However, the realities that exist in such cases offer much food for thought. It may well be that, in order to remain viable, every social system has to keep more information than it can integrate or justify – in exactly the same way as individuals, through unconscious processes of repression, take care that certain information that they hold and use is not accessible to other parts of their personality.

*The limits of consolidation.* By comparison with informal structures that are not endowed with a clear objective, the formal organization keeps things under control, because it sets out those decisive norms that everyone who wants to remain a member of the organization has to accept. The formal organization has at its disposal the most important instrument for enforcing a normative closed shop, that is, control over the decisions as to who comes in and who leaves.

Groups that have no effective control over membership in their areas of concern, but are obliged to cooperate with people who violate, discredit, and disregard their norms, find themselves hamstrung from the start. They cannot control those benefits of membership that motivate individuals to come and go. That is why they also cannot, *as groups*, "escape" from the administration – something that is possible for independent organizations. They are not even able to define their behavioral expectations in clear-cut terms as binding premises for decisions on entry or exit. Therefore, in the case of conflict, their norms, role allocations, and sanctions lack the necessary force. Their expectations are accepted simply as a matter of convenience or for the sake of peace, because people want to make use of the group as a suitable medium for their work. This, however, applies only because – and so long as – they are, for other reasons, members of the administration.

## Functions of Spontaneous Ordering

*No clear reference to tasks associated with official administrative positions.* We have already described the tasks associated with official administrative positions and designated them as a mer e extract from the total reality of expectations and actions. Spontaneous ordering provides for the inclusion of such extracts in the totality of a cooperative system of human action.

Classical organization theory believed that everything that was necessary for performing tasks could be labeled as a "means" and as such was subordinate to them. From a strictly logical vantage point, this is correct, but it is neither very conducive to understanding the actual behavior that occurs in an organization, nor satisfactory in scientific terms. If collaboration between people is to succeed and endure within a system of lasting cooperation, it has to fulfill rather complex requirements that cannot be reduced to a single formulation. It may be entirely sensible to proclaim a single objective or a cohesive group of tasks as the mission of an organization and to work hard for its realization. At the same time, however, this obscures the fact that other, incompatible needs must be satisfied. Thus, the mission statement is indeed a norm of administrative action, but it does not offer a theory of the reality of administration.

The functions of spontaneous ordering in administrative systems cannot be grasped as means to an end. Spontaneous behavioral ordering attaches itself to the problems that arise from those situations where people experience tension resulting from being forced to cooperate in an unbalanced, one-sided commitment to very specific achievements. Bureaucracies that were not conducted according to the same strict performance requirements that prevailed in the administration of industrial states, but instead merely had to administer their own social standing – such as the bureaucracy of old Siam

– were entirely at ease with formal acts and did not need any informal ordering. Conversely, this comparison demonstrates that in formal behavior and its social organization we have compensatory processes of a one-sided, rationally structured performance system.

*The fulfillment of non-authorized tasks.* Since the meaning of spontaneous measures is not made explicit, or made explicit only in confidential relationships, these measures are suitable as solutions to follow-up problems, which inevitably result from official tasks, but are not in keeping with the ideals associated with such tasks. They are known as behavioral intricacies, secret recipes, or business-facilitating tricks. Often they are seen as the "characteristics" of particular people or professional groups, such as lawyers, office managers, or town planners. As such, they therefore appear in a more or less distorted, opaque form. The functions of spontaneous measures, which wrestle with such seemingly unnecessary pressures on a daily basis, remain for the most part latent. In consequence, the prevailing ideology of official tasks is and remains protected.

Attempts to uncover the latent functions of

spontaneous action essentially bring to light two reasons for this state of affairs, both of which we have already encountered. On the one hand, there is the discrepancy between the fulfillment of tasks and the self-image of the system, and on the other, there is the discrepancy between the organization's interests and personal interests.

*The absorption of uncertainty.* The production of good decisions presupposes more intensive communication than can be made apparent in the written decision itself. For this reason, the paths of formal communication, which actually consist merely of chains of intermediary decisions that have been made on the basis of full responsibility, do not suffice to create true cooperation in the case of difficult decisions. Discussion is an indispensable means of administration. The liveliness and productivity of a discussion depend, however, not only on the possession of information and the intelligence and expressiveness of one's partner, but also on certain social conditions, especially trust and a spontaneously settled code of conduct.

The preparatory exchange of opinions has to process the fact that no decision is as certain as it pretends to be and that the information that is at the disposal of an administration, or which can be acquired without incurring exorbitant costs, hardly ever suffices to provide ultimate certitude. Therefore, spontaneous discussion not only has the purpose of stimulating and gathering all the information and ideas that are within the administration's reach. It also serves to create consensus and absorb those inevitable remnants of uncertainty that cannot be preempted by means of rational decision-making techniques.[5]

*The absorption of conflicts.* According to official guidance, all conflicts in an administration can and must be decided formally. If no solution is to be found on the basis of rational argumentation, the decision falls to the next-highest common superior. Such formal controversies are conducted in the open. People who succeed in associating their personal goals with those of the organization, and who are skilled in bringing their vehicle close to the filling station of admissible arguments, may also be able to expedite their own advancement through such conflicts. In actual fact, however, it is out of the question for all disagreements to be processed through official channels. Many topics are too sensitive for such a procedure; for example, if one has reservations over the promotion of a colleague or if one wants to air vague suspicions about his references. To be sure, even those controversies that would be appropriately dealt with through the official channel would hopelessly clog it up without some pre-sorting.

In order to unburden the official channel, there is the formal obligation first to seek an understanding with the colleague in question. Here too, a wealth of informal conflict-resolution methods play a part in this process. These include:

- providing incomplete information only;
- taking one's unsuspecting opponent by surprise;
- exploiting absences and temporary replacements;
- offering a quid pro quo;
- controlling the situation by invoking one's own personal rank and, not least, one's good working relationships should one's partners shows an especially strong interest in an issue, so making it difficult to say "No."

In addition, there are the more far-reaching forms for the preemptive treatment of conflicts that make sure that putative opponents, firstly, will not reach certain positions, or otherwise that they will not remain there for very long, or, at the very least, that their authority, their financial means, and their access to their superior will be cut back. In the final analysis, all of these interventions cannot replace the official channel as the last conduit of contention, but they can provide relief and absorb causes of conflict to such a degree that the official channel, in many instances, is used only to ratify a compromise that has already been reached, or to confirm with grand ceremony a victory that has already been achieved.

Informal conflicts are anything but savage quarrels. They do not undermine the general order, although many a participant presumably emerges from them with paralyzed vitality. These conflicts are kept within limits through spontaneously evolving reference points and, above all, the necessity of continued collaboration with one's opponents. In this case as well, the highest norm is that all participants have to observe the minimal conditions for the continuation of their membership of the organization. Depending on the circumstances, this may turn out to be a tactical advantage, an obstacle, or even a trap.

As a result of this rule, informal conflicts have to be conducted under cover. Their invisibility has two significant advantages. It makes it possible for losers to remain in their positions without losing face; they can pretend that nothing has happened at all. In addition, it also activates a wealth of conflict-resolution techniques in an administration without the need ever officially to admit their existence.

*Facilitating personal adaptation.* Finally, spontaneous ordering also serves to facilitate personal adaptation to the formally regulated, thoroughly rationalized work regime of an administration.

Among the strategies of personal adaptation to an organization one may find the following:

- the strategy of personal indifference to one's duty by taking enjoyable secret breaks;
- the strategy of personalizing one's workplace, of room decoration;
- the strategy of subtle self-promotion at the practical work level;

- the strategy of good deeds that will require thanks;
- the strategy of advancing to prestigious, highly visible positions.

No matter which of these adaptation strategies individuals may choose, they have to presuppose for all of them complementary roles of shared experience, recognition, support, and enmity. It is spontaneous ordering that secures the complementary nature of these unofficial roles, in order to make sure that in one's personal actions one does not operate in a vacuum.

# Subtervision or The Art of Directing Superiors

## I

"Subtervision": a new word and a strange topic. Therefore, let me start with a few words that explain how I came to it. My professional career led me from a work environment that was, so to speak, defined by the presence of superiors to one almost entirely devoid of any superiors. In the process, I suddenly began to feel that something was missing – and not just the strong shoulder that occasionally offers support and makes itself available for a good cry. Superiors do not just provide protection and consolation. They are also an important tool that can be deployed in multifarious ways so as to bring one's plans and objectives to fruition. In so far as they are actively engaged, those who live without superiors have to rely on themselves alone in the widely differing situations in which they seek to promote their interests. If you have a superior you can concentrate your relationship efforts on him without wasting your time and energy on having to deal with difficult people. You can, so to speak, make your superior the focal point and invest your energy in this relationship and then use the power provided by this relationship, without necessarily relieving him of this annoyance of having to deal with these people. Of course, a concentration of opportunities also brings with it a concentration of risks. Many managers turn out to be uncooperative, difficult, or simply incompetent to such a degree that it would be better to hold the reins in your own hands. Apart from this personal aspect, there are also a great many structurally determined variables that have not been topics for research, but that are crucial for any understanding of both the meaning and the success of one's dealings with superiors.

Furthermore, there is a second motive for this

lecture. I simply find it unjust that managers, who are already privileged by their position, are in addition supported by scientific research, favored with courses about leadership, and equipped with corresponding techniques, whereas lower-level employees, who are structurally unprivileged, have to make do without any such help. What is more, dealing with managers is certainly no easier than dealing with such employees. To be sure, no scientific analysis will ever prevent employees from occasionally fearing their managers. It may, however, bring them to the point where they will be able to draw the right conclusions from their fear.

Finally, I would like to add one last introductory remark. There is no pertinent literature and no empirical research available on the topic I have chosen. Yet I hope to be able to show that there are a number of insights in the area of general sociological research on organizations that can be applied to our topic. I think that I shall, therefore, also be able to give you an impression of the potential of organizational analysis, which is quite abstract and makes its intervention at a rather theoretical level. This would be the third motive – in fact, the main motive – for this lecture.

# II

Hierarchies have a distorting effect on judgments and even on perceptions. The door behind which the president sits is different from the one behind which a modest employee sits. The secretary of state who is forced to retire pretty much wears the loss of his office on his sleeve. First, you must dissociate yourself from this immediate, structurally conditioned impression. In the process, it can help greatly if you imagine that the boss in question is wearing no clothes.

More useful – because the starting point is more abstract – is to question the time and capacity for conscious decision-making at someone's disposal. The central point of departure for modern organizational theory is that shortage of consciousness is an anthropological constant that is not capable of being expanded. Superiors cannot be exempted from this strict law. Their concentration also has limits, and their day too consists of no more than twenty-four hours. One's rise in a hierarchy does not provide one with more awareness or a higher capacity for concentration. If one observes from this perspective the typical construction of a hierarchy, it becomes apparent that simply in terms of capacity, the center of gravity for conscious decision-making must lie in the lower ranks and that constraints on time and attentiveness originate in the upper echelons.

# III

This much is universally valid. If we now pay closer attention to the positions and perspectives of subordinates, we must first ask what their goals might be. We can pick out two of them. On the one side, there are goals relating to self-presentation – attempts to appear as the person that you would like to be. In the long term, this includes the advancement of one's own career as a way of achieving those jobs where you can actually be who you want to be.

On the other side, there are strategies for influencing decisions. Certain interests group around the subordinate employee's job, for example the interests of a particular division or department. But there is also the interest in having sufficient time to make decisions or exercise control over critical variables, as well as the interest in a stock of excuses and apologies to be deployed when mistakes are made. In general, all these interests will be realized only by influencing certain decisions. Such interests may be related more or less closely to specific tasks.

For both groups of goals – self-presentation and influencing decisions – the following two questions arise. To what degree are they integrated in the sense that pursuing one of these goals is instrumental in achieving the other, and vice versa? Secondly, who is the relevant audience for these strategies? That is, does the superior constitute the relevant audience for both of these goals, self-presentation and influencing decisions, or do one's colleagues or perhaps even one's own subordinates constitute the relevant audience? To the extent that one's superior, as an individual, constitutes the relevant audience, integration succeeds. For only in this case do self-presentation and influencing decisions coincide. In the other cases, integration is not impossible, but it is more problematic.

# IV

Let us turn, then, to the issue of power relations.[1] Here, too, as in the case of hierarchies, it is first of all a matter of diminishing optical illusions. Perhaps one's first thought is that in the relationship between superior and subordinate, it is the superior who has the power – at least predominantly. However, this is not necessarily the case. At the very least, it cannot be decided merely on the basis of presupposition without further examination.

In the first place, it will be necessary to determine an appropriate concept of power despite all those difficulties with the theory of power. Using the concept of power, I would like to summarize the process of transferring selection operations.[2] The following restrictive conditions need to be taken into consideration:

- selection and transfer take place through decisions, and their acceptance occurs in the face of alternatives that are to be avoided;
- subordinates accept decisions because they want to avoid sanctions;
- superiors accept decisions because the

alternative – forming their own judgment – would be too much of an effort.

On this basis, it is clear that the superior may have power over the subordinate and also the subordinate may have power over the superior.

Organization sociologists have known for a long time that the distribution of power in a system is not captured simply by a hierarchical model. Nevertheless, understanding reciprocal relations of power remains a difficult task. The classical theory of power took its paradigm from the image of physical forces. Mutual blocking had to be prevented. Whoever has more power has all the power, because in cases of conflict he is the one who prevails. In contrast to this view, one needs to recognize that there are different kinds of power to which this kind of calculation cannot be applied.

The power of the superior rests on the possibility of making formal decisions about conflicts and of presenting a subordinate with the alternative to his membership – which is to say, of threatening him with dismissal. The power of the subordinate rests on the complexity of the situation within which the superior has to make a decision. This requires help in decision-making, which is dependent upon pre-sorting. Superiors would be lost if their subordinates were to pass all problems upward. Ironically, the power of subordinates over their superiors also rests on the formal organization, that is, on superiors' duties and responsibilities and the right of subordinates to obtain decisions from their leadership.

Apart from that, the distribution of power in individual cases of course varies. It depends on the degree of complexity and uncertainties of the situation surrounding the superior's decision, as well as on the degree to which the superior can ensure success through formal decisions.

In order to understand this analysis, it is imperative that you familiarize yourselves with a somewhat unusual thesis: Power can be executed effectively only in the form of cooperation, and not in the form of conflict. After all, at stake is the process of transferring selection operations – a common procedure in decision-making. In fact, open conflicts between superiors and subordinates are rare and always imply a collapse of power relations. Power on both sides can be increased through trust-based cooperation.

Sabotage, by contrast, leads to immobility and can, at best, make sense in political, but never in bureaucratic, terms. Such a system becomes self-stabilizing by a process in which each side, in the interest of its own particular power over the other, takes into consideration the other's power and refrains from doing harm to it.

I still have to cover two major themes – with very little time left. In the first place, I wanted to introduce to you a number of system variables that are important for the relationship between superior and subordinate (part V), and then I wanted to give a demonstration of an analysis of specific situations and the strategic possibilities through which such a relationship takes shape, produces its own history, and – depending on the circumstances – may assume forms that can be reversed only with the utmost difficulty (part VI). Let us begin with an overview of some important structural variables.

# V

One of these variables is the distribution of outside contacts, specifically regarding input and output. At which hierarchical level does impact from the outside world occur? And at what level does the outside world (a further question would be: Which outside world?) affect the system? Such external relations are of course mirrored in the tensions between superiors and subordinates.

In this connection, we also ought to ask about the distribution of initiatives within the system. This ought to correlate, in my view, with external contacts, since otherwise one would end up with a faulty organization whose ability to achieve an equilibrium with its external world would be questionable. Moreover, how close are these initiatives to the decision process? How much is definitely ruled out? Are initiatives programmed or not?

A third issue, in addition to external contacts and the right to start initiatives, concerns the distribution of relevant uncertainties within the system. At what level is uncertainty absorbed? In government agencies that ought to plan ahead, but cannot do so, this typically happens at too low a level. Just think of what happens in ministries of culture or development aid. Responsibility slips downward. Decisions are made at a low level and the superiors are reduced to playing a mediating role – a fact that generates resignation among subordinates rather than enjoyment of their power.

Moreover, one ought to consider relationships among the subordinates themselves. Usually, a superior is in charge of a number of subordinates. When subordinates begin to deal with their superior, it is scarcely avoidable that these subordinates will meet and recognize one another as colleagues. What kind of relationship do we have here? Presumably, this is closely associated with the target structure – a topic that is of great importance for leadership theories, yet still has to be worked out for the theory of subtervision.

The last group of questions concerns the supposed length of the relationship. When you start off, how long do you expect it to last? Who is really mobile: the superior or the subordinate? Who usually trains the other?

If you look at all of this together, you learn something about the limits of consciousness. An overview of all these connections is no longer achievable, or can only be achieved in relation to a concrete situation. Our schema serves their analysis, as a catalogue of bookmarks reminding us of all the things that have to be taken into account. Of course, the theoretical proposition goes far beyond this.

# VI

Now we come to our last point: the relative autonomy of situations. This issue, too, needs much more theoretical preparation than I can offer at the moment. Suffice it to say that in general terms, in all institutionally established systems or even highly organized systems, individual situations to a greater or lesser degree have an enormous amount of autonomy. Even if you have analyzed these large organizations, this alone does not allow you to keep a hold on the situation for very long. You still have to "bring your knowledge to bear" on it. Even situations involving several participants are social systems that are open to sociological analysis. There are situations that go smoothly and others that "go belly-up." If you look closely and bring together your observations, perhaps after a period of time, and perhaps also after some experiments on specific matters, you will eventually find out that certain rules apply.

Rules governing success in specific situations are also, at the same time, points of departure for strategies of varying subtlety. I should like to illustrate this with a few examples.

- Respect, as the formal recognition of a role of higher rank, is of course important. In this context, people are quite often worried by the problem of servility. It is, however, possible to express defiance in a respectful way, for instance presenting oneself as an uncomprehending or bored listener. The supreme norm is tact. One has to treat others as they would like to be treated. In other words, you have to capture and reflect the other's intended self-presentation in your own actions. Time and again, I have tried to experiment at the limits of tactlessness. It does not pay off. One may cause confusion, introduce a slight tremor into the situation, perhaps even cause a sufficiently strong disturbance to shift attention away from an unpleasant topic. To achieve much more than this is not possible.
- Tact is of particular importance in situations in which others are not at all free to choose their own self-presentations. Such situations

are common for superiors who do not have this freedom, but have to present themselves as dominant, decisive, and lofty. Especially in the case of ostensibly weak people, tactlessness is not only cruel, but typically also meets with disapproval from others. One must act in much more subtle ways.

• A special problem lies in the difference between starring and directorial roles. It requires a complex management of visible and invisible influences. Conferences are one type of such special situations. Here, the superior has to act with relatively little advice. He can have all the necessary technical details presented to him, but not the big line of the argument. It may well happen that, without noticing it, he departs from this line, or the situation develops altogether differently than had been planned – *Don Carlos* to *Charley's Aunt*.[3] In general, there are no firm prescriptions; there is merely the difference between small tricks and the big line. It is simply not possible to direct superiors by giving them a guarantee for an individual case, which runs contrary to the expectation that such a guarantee is expected to be given by the superior to his subordinates. One must keep superiors on a long lead, as it were. If on occasions they break free, this cannot be avoided.

But let us return to general situations and offer one more example of a more abstract consideration, that concerning the time structure. Interactions between superiors and subordinates are thematically concentrated encounters. For this reason, a synchronization of experience is necessary in spite of their very different experiences of time. For some, everything proceeds too slowly and they are always in danger of straying from the path. For others, everything proceeds too fast and, in situations where they are obliged to act, they end up being pressed for time. So they cannot think things through properly, and only in retrospect do they understand what they have done.

The distribution of time is not just a matter of talent; it may also be altered through preparation. One must keep in mind that precisely because of this issue, the right to dispense time goes to the superior. It is he who determines the speed and duration of meetings, and the points in time when they take place. Yet formal authority is always sluggish; it is not possible to constantly tell a fast-thinking employee to "Slow down."

Choosing a counter-rhythm is again enervating. Small gains can be made, for instance, by expressing oneself in a complicated way. By the time others have understood, they will have missed the moment for voicing objections. Accordingly, one may respond as follows to a request to attend a meeting: "I'll see whether I can to find an appropriate moment to convince myself that it's necessary to show up."

# VII

Yet is all of this not a rather dangerous enterprise? Will it not undermine all order? Does this not abrogate all basic ethical convictions and replace them, at best, with mere analytical intelligence?

Here are the answers to these questions:

1 Our problem is not a matter of staying true to some principle, but of analytically unlocking complex facts and circumstances. To this purpose, our diagnostic abilities must be improved, and for this, there is simply more time and more potential at the lower levels of a hierarchy than at the higher ones.

2 This game can anyway be played at all levels of a hierarchy – even at the very top – as far as there are superiors to hand.

3 As soon as this game becomes transparent, it can be played in reverse.

4 Finally, the system can defend itself in entirely legitimate ways – namely, by promoting an employee who tries to direct his superiors, and making him the new boss.

# Afterword

*Jürgen Kaube*

The ethnography of executive floors – if it is indeed a matter of floors – has hardly been developed. We do not have a sociology of the board meeting, the crisis phone call, or the ante-room. We do, however, know a few things about industrial administration, mid-level managers, stockbrokers, and even the uniformed doormen of the buildings in which bosses reside.[1] Research on elites assumes that it knows the social background of elites, even though it most often limits the concept of "elite" to business leaders and disregards the bosses of churches, legal courts, sports associations, and government authorities. We also know much about the functions of hierarchies, power, and management – which is to say, about structures that are assumed to exist, if there are to be bosses. Yet due to the lack of participant observation, about the behavioral problems found at the top of organizations we have little knowledge that is not tainted by the considerable disadvantages typical of interviews, biographies, and the kind of reports that are used by first-hand witnesses to let off steam.[2] Moreover, bosses only very rarely conduct any research into their roles. To be sure, they invest a lot of time observing other bosses, but such observation is dominated by their own career considerations.[3] Therefore, the question, "What do bosses do?" still leads us into largely uncharted territory.[4]

Niklas Luhmann was no boss either. Otherwise, how could he have created his oeuvre? Moreover, in one of the contributions to this volume, he refers to the period that was to become the longest phase of his intellectual life as an exceptional case of a manager-free existence. All of this is to say that the university adds further obstacles to gaining insight into the sociology of bosses, precisely because hardly any are to be found within its confines, least of all in the social sciences.

Nevertheless, no one can read these essays by

Luhmann without immediately having a sense of their empirical background. Very much like his great book, *Funktionen und Folgen formaler Organisation*[5] of 1964, these essays, which were written in the same context, do more than just condense an enormous amount of reading in the sociology of organizations. They also consolidate Luhmann's experiences over eight years, from 1954 onward, as a higher civil servant in Lower Saxony – the motivation for his move into sociological theory. These included experiences such as the nervousness of an administration when a change of leadership was impending; the disposition of civil servants to act in a strategic way, resulting from the fact that their work was personally attributed to them; the demonstration of inequality through the communication of equality when bosses address their subordinates as if they were colleagues; the techniques of subtervision, including such stratagems as the avoidance of objections by means of complicated communication at decisive moments, or the communication of defiance right at the very limits of respect by giving the appearance of boredom.

Luhmann captured such impressions solely as asides and did not pour them into the mold of a handbook on the scope for role-playing in modern organizations.[6] He did not put the final touches to the manuscript of his lecture on the art of directing managers, which explicitly holds out the prospect of help for subordinates and thus, by implication, provides, as it were, for management consultancy from below. It was published for the first time in the German edition of this book. To be sure, Luhmann's suggestions regarding the particularities, on the one hand, of administrations as opposed to industrial companies, and, on the other, of specific situations as opposed to those organizational structures that include the managerial role, do not lend themselves to being turned into concrete prescriptions for bosses and those who are affected by them.

If one would like to derive practical conclusions from the insights that are presented here, one would do well to define the specifics of one's own situation by means of the concepts that Luhmann offers. Thus, referring to the significance of self-presentation in organizations, he points out the difference between those areas that are predominantly communicative and those that also include manual labor. Today one would also distinguish between bosses and organizations that have a high public visibility and those in which the media are less interested (and which, in turn, are less interested in the media). Furthermore, organizations with a high density of regulations suggest different forms of interaction between managers and employees than those where unpredictability is a feature of what is wanted from those who contribute to the operations of organizations. These include advertising agencies, theaters, and newspapers. Wherever the presentation of individuality becomes a part of the required roles – as, for instance, in artistic creations or at the pinnacle of political parties – one must make allowances for the bosses and their charisma in ways that are quite different, say, from the retail trade or tax authorities.

If, as Luhmann emphasizes, power can be exercised only in the form of cooperation and not in that of conflict, flat hierarchies have different consequences for the boss's role than long official channels. If those channels are short instead, many more conflicts will end up on the boss's plate. In turn, the boss may prefer states of emergency to mask everything else, because this allows him to forget about the normal state of the organization and the actual stress tests that come with it. A further distinctive effect of different hierarchical levels concerns possibilities for promotion and shapes the leeway available to managers and their counterparts, as well as the financial circumstances of their ambitions.[7] Or let us simply take a structure that Luhmann does not include – namely, a structure with not just one boss, but several of equal rank who decide not just for their own area of competence, but on everything, through consensus, indifference, and exchanges.

Examples such as this make it clear that the practical benefits of these essays depend more on adopting their perspective than on trying to apply some of their observations to individual cases. The perspective in question is the result of Luhmann's reflections on the basic concepts of sociology during its golden American period. In the present context this involves especially such concepts as "role," "informal communication," and "hierarchy." Thus, thinking through the practical consequences of the trivial fact that the "boss" is both a role and a person in that role would prevent many short circuits on both sides of hierarchical communication. Often personal qualities that are ascribed to managers – such as flightiness, self-contradiction, and moodiness – may turn out to be mere accompanying effects of the bosses' role performance. Luhmann alludes to this when he speaks of the bosses' "accessible hours" (p. 60), which alternate with those when they are inaccessible. New bosses, in turn, learn that their feeling of having remained their old self is of little help to them in their new role, even when opponents who are long familiar with the person experience uncertainty, above all else, about that new role. Conversely, as a high-level civil servant once put it, where there is a failure to reflect on the fact that top positions tend to nour-ish and develop only certain of their occupants' personality traits, this leads to greater distance and contempt than is necessary. Whether con-flicts outlast a change of roles from colleague to boss, because the one is already committed to a particular opinion regarding the other, depends largely on the degree to which both sides tend to take things personally.

Luhmann's most important reflection in this context concerns spontaneous action. For Luhmann it requires not worrying beforehand about the likely approval of one's actions, or considering the image one is likely to project if one acts in that way. This, however, is possible only where the danger of embarrassing oneself is averted by the cognitive attitude of those who observe one's actions and do not take it personally if mistakes are made. Luhmann repeatedly discusses elements of collegial behavior, such as tact, self-discipline, the willingness to keep one's feelings to oneself, and mutual respect. In doing so he also touches upon the necessary preconditions of factually oriented communication in organizations, "whose social impact," as he puts it, "has not been considered" (p. 52). Such communication is unlikely to occur when the boss is present, because "restraint seems appropriate in interactions with him" (p. 59). Nonetheless, it is in the interest of most organizations to make spontaneous action possible. Perhaps this requirement can reconcile bosses to the organizational paradox that they are as indispensable, on the one hand, as they are disruptive, on the other.

# Sources of the Texts

"The New Boss." Published in *Verwaltungsarchiv* 53 (1962), pp. 11–24.

"The Spontaneous Creation of Order." Published in *Verwaltung: Eine einführende Darstellung*, edited by Fritz Morstein Marx in collaboration with Erich Becker and Carl Hermann Ule (Berlin: Duncker & Humblot GmbH, 1965), pp. 163–83.

"Subtervision or The Art of Directing Superiors." Previously unpublished typescript from Luhmann's papers, edited for this publication by Jürgen Kaube.

# Notes

## The New Boss

1 See, for instance, Erving Goffman, *The Presentation of Self in Everyday Life* (Edinburgh: University of Edinburgh, 1958; second edn.), pp. 4ff.; Ralph M. Stogdill, *Individual Behavior and Group Achievement* (New York, NY: Oxford University Press, 1959), pp. 96f.

2 Thus, for instance, Harvey Leibenstein, *Economic Theory and Organizational Analysis* (New York, NY: Harper and Brothers, 1960), p. 201.

3 This is stressed by Oskar Grusky, "Administrative Succession in Formal Organizations," *Social Forces* 39 (1960), pp. 105–15, here pp. 105ff.

4 See Meyer Fortes, "The Structure of Unilineal Descent Groups," *American Anthropologist* 55 (1953), pp. 17–41, here p. 36. For a further elaboration of this thought, see Siegfried F. Nadel, *The Theory*

*of Social Structure* (Glencoe, IL: Free Press, 1957), pp. 68f.

5 Melville Dalton, *Men Who Manage* (New York, NY: John Wiley, 1959), p. 234.

6 Fritz J. Roethlisberger and William J. Dickson saw this as one reason for the resistance of the informal order to formal changes. Ever since, this topic has been discussed frequently. See Fritz J. Roethlisberger and William J. Dickson, *Management and the Worker* (Cambridge, MA: Harvard University Press, 1939), p. 567.

7 *Translators' note:* In fact Luhmann writes here "Jeder läßt sein Visier so weit herunter," that is, "Each lowers his visor." This is surely a confusion on his part, as it is clear that what he means is that both sides leave their faces exposed, which has to involve raising their visor. We have translated this accordingly.

8 A similar list was compiled by Grusky, "Administrative Succession" (see note 3).

9 On a case in which such a change was not recognized as legitimate and which eventually led to a strike, see Alvin W. Gouldner, *Wildcat Strike: A Study in Worker–Management Relationships* (Yellow Springs, OH: Antioch Press, 1954), esp. pp. 79f. and 158.

10 See C. Roland Christensen, *Management Succession in Small and Growing Enterprises* (Boston, MA: Division of Research, Graduate School of Business Administration, Harvard University, 1953), and Donald B. Trow, "Executive Succession in Small Companies," *Administrative Science Quarterly* 6 (1961), pp. 228–39.

11 Grusky, "Administrative Succession" (see note 3), pp. 107 and 114f.

12 Gouldner, *Wildcat Strike* (see note 9), pp. 119ff. and 176ff.

See also Gouldner, *Patterns of Industrial Bureaucracy* (Glencoe, IL: Free Press, 1954), pp. 157ff.

13 As pointed out by Grusky, "Administrative Succession" (see note 3), pp. 108f. Also compare the discussion of both alternatives in Richard O. Carlson, "Succession and Performance among School Superintendents," *Administrative Science Quarterly* 6 (1961), pp. 201–27.

14 Georg Simmel, *Soziologie: Untersuchungen über die Formen der Vergesellschaftung* (Munich: Duncker & Humblot, 1923; 3rd, rev. edn.), pp. 509ff.

15 This was also pointed out by Gouldner, *Wildcat Strike* (see note 9), p. 157.

16 Such cataclysms of the informal system of communication on the occasion of a change in leadership have been observed frequently. See Roethlisberger and Dickson, *Management and the Worker* (see note 6), p. 453; Grusky, "Administrative Succession" (see note 3), p. 108; Gouldner, *Patterns of Industrial Bureaucracy* (see note 12), pp. 84f., and *Wildcat Strike* (see note 9), pp. 136f. and 157; Herman M. Somers, "The Federal Bureaucracy and the Change of Administration," *The American Political Science Review* 48 (1954), pp. 131–51, here pp. 145 and 147f.

17 Laurin L. Henry, *Presidential Transitions* (Washington, DC: Brookings Institution, 1960), pp. 541f.

18 See, e.g., Dalton, *Men Who Manage* (see note 5), pp. 28 and 62; Eli Ginzberg, *What Makes an Executive?* (New York, NY: Columbia University Press, 1955), p. 156; Norman H. Martin and Anselm L. Strauss, "Patterns of Mobility within Industrial Organizations," *The Journal of Business* 29 (1956), pp. 101–10, here p. 106.

19 On the problem of such "old lieutenants" see Gouldner, *Patterns of Industrial Bureaucracy* (see note 12), pp. 74ff.

20 Grusky, "Administrative Succession" (see note 3), p. 108, states that internal appointments in general create fewer difficulties. R. Stewart, "Management Succession," *The Manager* 23 (1955), pp. 579–82 and 676–9, here p. 580, is undecided on the matter.

21 *Translators' note:* The reference is to Daphne du Maurier's famous novel *Rebecca* of 1938, which Gouldner uses to illustrate a problem in industrial management. In the novel, as he states, "a young woman [...] married a widower, only to be plagued by the memory of his first wife, whose virtues were still widely extolled. One may suspect that many a past plant manager is, to some extent, idealized by the workers, even if disliked while present." Gouldner, *Patterns of Industrial Bureaucracy* (see note 12), pp. 79–83, here p. 79 n. 3.

22 See Grusky, "Administrative Succession" (see note 3), p. 107.

23 On the problems and techniques of such self-presentations see Goffman, *The Presentation of Self in Everyday Life* (see note 1).

24 In fact, this reaction is frequently mentioned in the existing literature. See Roethlisberger and Dickson, *Management and the Worker* (see note 6), pp. 452f.; Gouldner, *Patterns of Industrial Bureaucracy* (see note 12), pp. 59ff.; Carlson, "Succession and Performance among School Superintendents" (see note 13), p. 216; Grusky, "Administrative Succession" (see note 3), p. 109; and Grusky, "Role Conflict in Organizations: A Study of Prison Camp Officials," *Administrative Science Quarterly* 3 (1959), pp. 452–72, here pp. 463ff.

25 Much evidence for these claims can be found in Conrad M. Arensberg (ed.), *Research in Industrial Human Relations: A*

*Critical Appraisal* (New York, NY: Harper, 1957); see also John M. Pfiffner and Frank P. Sherwood, *Administrative Organization* (Englewood Cliffs, NJ: Prentice Hall, 1960), esp. pp. 364ff.

## The Spontaneous Creation of Order

*Translators' note:* The German subtitle of this text, "Der Mensch in der Verwaltung," is obviously a reference to Albert Camus's *L'homme révolté*, which appeared in 1951 and was translated into German as *Der Mensch in der Revolte* in 1953.

1 William Foote Whyte, "Small Groups and Large Organizations," in: John R. Rohrer and Muzafer Sherif (eds.), *Social Psychology at the Crossroads* (New York, NY: Harper, 1951), pp. 297–312.

2 The postal workers' union had great difficulty in July 1962 in conceiving *Aktion Igel* [Plan Hedgehog], a nationwide work-to-rule, as a program for industrial action, forcing it down workers' throats, and putting it into effect. As a "natural experiment" of sorts, it showed quite nicely how far removed from actual life situations was this attempted reduction to formal duties. Such duties had to be identified and extracted from the realities of everyday behavior by means of an entirely artificial operation. It takes a considerable effort to impose it in the form of a work-to-rule. *Translators' note: Aktion Igel* was a nationwide work-to-rule by German postal workers in 1962. The idea was to demonstrate what a postal service by the book – without the additional informal input and the effort of the postal workers above and beyond what was explicitly required of them – would look like and thereby to make a case

for higher salaries. The name of the work-to-rule (which, incidentally, was not called a "strike" by the union) was an allusion to the well-known German folktale of the hare and the hedgehog, which the Brothers Grimm included in their famous collection of fairytales. According to a series of accounts from different German cities that were published under the title "Die Post zeigte ihre Stacheln ..." ["The postal service revealed its quills ..."] in the German weekly *Die Zeit* of July 6, 1962, the work-to-rule was unsuccessful precisely because separating the workers' formally prescribed work from their informal input not only proved exceedingly difficult, but also led to a number of paradoxical results. See http://www.zeit.de/1962/27/die-post-zeigte-ihre-stacheln/komplettansicht.

3 Harold E. Dale, *The Higher Civil Service of Great Britain* (London: Oxford University Press, 1941), p. 37.

4 Those who do not appreciate this – for instance, lonesome intellectuals – not only isolate themselves, but also unsettle the collegial cooperation that creates mutual respect by deriving their own standards of respect from the outside, for instance from academic circles or professional groups, or simply from the recognition they receive from the actual clients of the administration.

5 The need for non-rational foundations for decisions grows exactly to the degree that decisions cannot be programmed in sufficient detail, or at all. At higher levels, especially at the leadership level of an administration, this need can be felt almost incessantly, and it imposes itself especially in instances when the administration has to adjust its decision process to rapidly changing environmental conditions – for example, in administrative branches that are politically exposed.

## Subtervision

1 *Translators' note:* Certain words and phrases in this chapter – which was clearly intended (or given) as a talk – were inserted by Jürgen Kaube, who edited Luhmann's unpublished manuscript and filled in the gaps that Luhmann had left. In the German text these insertions appear in square brackets, but this has the unintended consequence of breaking up the text and so making it difficult to read. We have, therefore, simply incorporated them into the text, but wish readers to be aware that words have been added on occasions to provide sense and coherence.

2 *Translators' note:* The German original reads "Selektionsleitungen," that is, "selection guidance," which is slightly awkward, but not impossible. However, four paragraphs down, we encounter "Übertragung von Selektionsleistungen," that is, "transferring selection operations," which makes a typo the most convincing explanation for "Selektionsleitungen" here.

3 *Translators' note:* The references are to Friedrich Schiller's classic tragedy *Don Carlos* of 1787 (on which Verdi later based his eponymous opera) and Brandon Thomas's cross-dressing farce *Charley's Aunt* of 1892, which was later filmed more than once. Two film versions, one of 1955 with the popular actor Heinz Rühmann in the lead, the other of 1963 with the Viennese singer-actor Peter Alexander, were especially successful in Germany at the time of Luhmann's writing.

# Afterword

1 Melville Dalton, *Men Who Manage: Fusions of Feeling and Theory in Administration* (New York, NY: John Wiley, 1959); Tony Watson, *In Search of Management: Culture, Chaos and Control in Managerial Work* (London: Routledge, 1994); Karen Z. Ho, *Liquidated: An Ethnography of Wall Street* (Durham, NC: Duke University Press, 2009); Peter Bearman, *Doormen* (Chicago, IL: University of Chicago Press, 2005).

2 For a recent example, see Katharina Münk, *Und morgen bringe ich ihn um: Als Chefsekretärin im Top-Management* [*And Tomorrow I am Going to Kill Him: An Executive Secretary Working in Top Management*] (Frankfurt am Main: Eichborn Verlag, 2006).

3 Cf. the one great exception offering a sociology of the executive floor: Robert Jackall, *Moral Mazes: The World of Corporate Managers* (Oxford: Oxford University Press, 1988).

4 Stephen Marglin, "What Do Bosses Do? The Origin and Function of Hierarchy in Capitalist Production," *Review of Radical Political Economics* 6 (1974), pp. 60–112, and 7 (1975), pp. 20–37.

5 Niklas Luhmann, *Funktionen und Folgen formaler Organisation* (Berlin: Duncker & Humblot, 1964).

6 *Translators' note*: Kaube's term "Handorakel" ["hand-book"] is a reference to the German translation of Baltasar Gracián's seminal *Oráculo Manual y Arte de Prudencia* [The Oracle: A Manual of the Art of Discretion].

7 For a very complex, but ultimately rather perplexed account see Georges Perec, *L'art et la manière d'aborder son chef de service pour lui demander une augmentation*

(Paris: Hachette littératures, 2008) [Kaube cites the German translation, *Über die Kunst, seinen Chef anzusprechen und ihn um eine Gehaltserhöhung zu bitten* (Stuttgart: Klett-Cotta, 2010)].